Keeping with the Joneses

A Comedy

by John Chapman
and Jeremy Lloyd

A SAMUEL FRENCH ACTING EDITION

SAMUEL FRENCH

FOUNDED 1830

SAMUELFRENCH.COM

CAST

(in order of appearance)

DEIRDRE JONES
JOE
GEOFFREY JONES
GRINDLE
MRS. WAYNEFLETE
CLIVE PATEL
RAYMOND BLAKE
SONIA BLAKE
BOBBY

PLACE

The action of the play takes place in the underground atomic shelter beneath the back garden of a house in Northolt.

TIME

The present

KEEPING DOWN
WITH THE JONESES

ACT ONE
Scene One

The set is a fully equipped underground atomic shelter. It is taste-
fully furnished something in the manner of a suburban sub-
marine. The pipe is "T" shaped with a centre hallway with a
spiral staircase going up to the entrance hatch, right of the
hallway is a dining-room-cum-kitchen & to the left a recrea-
tion & radio communications room. Other rooms are at the
left end of the pipe, U.S.C. at the back of the hallway is a door
leading to bathroom & lavatory.

The curtain rises on a blacked-out stage. After a second there
is the sound of a heavy metal hatch opening.

DEIRDRE. These stairs are very steep.

JOE. I can't see a thing.

DEIRDRE. Don't worry, there's a light switch here
somewhere.

(Suddenly the set is bathed in light.)

JOE. Bloody 'ell!

(DEIRDRE JONES comes to the bottom of the stairs followed by JOE. DEIRDRE JONES is smartly & sensibly dressed. JOE is a good-looking young man wearing denims, training shoes & a leather jacket.)

DEIRDRE. That's where I want the phone, over there in the lounge. *(They walk through.)*

JOE. Mrs. Jones, when you asked for an extension you forgot to mention that it was halfway through to Australia.

DEIRDRE. Don't be silly, we're only 25 feet below ground.

JOE. But I've only brought six foot of cable. You'll need another hundred feet to go from here to the main box on your house.

DEIRDRE. I thought you carried a big roll around with you and cut off whatever you needed.

JOE. Yeah, but it's not in my pocket. It's in the van.

DEIRDRE. Can I have the phone or not?

JOE. Yes, now don't get excited. I'll get another hundred foot, connect it to that little box there, connect that to the phone and you'll be talking your head off in no time.

DEIRDRE. Thank you.

JOE. Pretty sprauncey, this shelter, is it for the whole road?

DEIRDRE. No, it's private, my husband's motto is "Be Prepared."

JOE. What's he expecting? World War Three?

DEIRDRE. Frankly yes.

(A figure comes down the stairs wearing wellingtons, a mackin-tosh, rubber gloves & a bathing cap, and a gas mask.)

JOE. *(in mock horror)* Blimy, it's started. *(There is a muffled sound from behind the gas mask.)*

DEIRDRE. Darling, we can't hear a word you're saying.

GEOFFREY. *(Removes his gas mask. He is earnest & over-efficient.)* Sorry Deirdre.

JOE. You expecting bad weather down here?

GEOFFREY. No, no, this is my nerve gas equipment.

JOE. Do you know something I don't.

GEOFFREY. One only has to read the papers.

JOE. There was nothing about it in "The Sun" this morning.

DEIRDRE. I think you can assume that my husband, being an M.P. knows a bit more than the newspapers.

JOE. An M.P.?

GEOFFREY. Of course I am, I'm your local M.P.

JOE. I've never seen you before.

DEIRDRE. Take off your bathing cap, Geoffrey.

GEOFFREY. What? Oh yes. *(He removes it.)* There you are.

DEIRDRE. Now do you recognize him?

JOE. No.

GEOFFREY. I'm Geoffrey Jones.

JOE. *(Looks at him.)* Cor, so you are. You look quite normal on your poster.

GEOFFREY. Who exactly are you?!

JOE. *(Holds up the phone.)* I'll give you a clue.

GEOFFREY. Ah, telephone engineer.

JOE. Got it in one, it's easy to see why you got the job.

DEIRDRE. Would you hurry up and connect that.

JOE. *(taking out form)* While I'm at it, how do you want your entry to be put in the phone book?

DEIRDRE. I don't, we'd like to be ex-directory.

JOE. Ah. You don't want anyone phoning for a reservation if things get nasty?

DEIRDRE. Well, we've already got the au pair girl, and of course my mother — apart from little Charles and my husband.

(GRINDLE, a beautiful Scandinavian au pair, appears at the top of the stairs in a short skirt. GRINDLE gingerly takes a step at a time down the spiral staircase with a carry cot.)

DEIRDRE. *(Walks out into the hall.)* Be careful, Grindle, you shouldn't wear stiletto heels to come down those stairs.

GRINDLE. I will take them off next time.

DEIRDRE. Yes, please do.

GRINDLE. *(By now she has arrived at the foot of stairs.)* Where am I putting the baby?

DEIRDRE. Straight through there *(indicating recreation room)* into the bedroom.

GEOFFREY. Give little Charles to me. *(GEOFFREY takes the cot into bedroom, GRINDLE walks past JOE & stops to adjust her ankle strap, then follows GEOFFREY.)*

JOE. *(admiringly)* Roll on World War Three.

DEIRDRE. Are you a married man?

Joe. No, but if I was I'd still fancy other birds.

Deirdre. I've seen too many marriages break down for that very reason.

Joe. Is that your problem then?

Deirdre. No, no, I'm speaking as a Marriage Guidance Councillor, my marriage has been particularly fortunate, my husband would never look at another woman.

Joe. *(looking at GRINDLE)* Who chose her then?

Deirdre. It was a joint decision, my husband agreed with me that she was the most promising girl we'd seen.

Joe. I'll go along with that.

Deirdre. You men are extraordinary, just from your tone of voice it's clear that all you are thinking about is sex.

Joe. Well we all do, let's face it.

Deirdre. My husband's beyond that stage of ogling a pretty girl, he looks at what's underneath.

Joe. *(with a wink)* Good place to start.

Deirdre. I have a lot to do, would you just finish the wiring?

Joe. First bit's done. Now what colour phone would you like? Black or white?

(GEOFFREY enters dressed normally.)

Deirdre. What colour phone, Geoffrey?

Geoffrey. I think we'd like green.

Deirdre. Yes, that would match beautifully.

Joe. I'll have to go back to the depot for that.

GEOFFREY. Be as quick as you can old chap, we batten down the hatch at midday sharp.

JOE. What do I do if I'm a bit late, knock?

GEOFFREY. No. Once that lid's down, it stays down.

JOE. How long for?

GEOFFREY. Well to make the trial as authentic as possible we'll all be down for 3 weeks.

JOE. Three weeks?!

DEIRDRE. All but a day.

GEOFFREY. Unfortunately we have to come up a day early as my office manager is getting married.

DEIRDRE. And my husband is the best man.

JOE. Hang on, if you're an M.P. what are you doing with an office?

GEOFFREY. I'm also an architect.

JOE. Oh, moon-lighting, eh?

GEOFFREY. Most M.P.'s have other jobs.

DEIRDRE. My husband's responsible for quite a lot of the architecture in this area.

JOE. Oh is he? Didn't have a hand in the Waverley Estate did he, by any chance?

DEIRDRE. Yes.

GEOFFREY. One of my first jobs, I won an Award for it.

JOE. You ought to try living in it mate.

DEIRDRE. I think it's very prettty, for what it is.

JOE. Pretty yes.

DEIRDRE. I was driving through it the other day and I noticed a lot of the houses had window boxes.

JOE. That's weeds growing out of the wet wood. Those houses were built on reclaimed land and on a quiet night you can hear them sucking it up like huge concrete sponges.

GEOFFREY. You're exaggerating.

JOE. Once I tell all my neighbors where you live, you'll be hiding down here a lot longer than three weeks. So long. *(He exits up the stairs.)*

DEIRDRE. Perhaps you shouldn't have told him about your award.

GEOFFREY. Why not? I was proud of it. I'm also proud of the fact that I put in this shelter and had the foresight to save the entire family and your mother from possible oblivion.

DEIRDRE. What do you mean "entire family *and* my mother?" Let's not forget that my mother paid for a good deal of this.

GEOFFREY. It's not exactly one-way traffic, is it? She's had our roof over her head for the past ten years and let's face it, it's not been too easy sharing a house with somebody who's living in another world.

DEIRDRE. She's perfectly coherent.

GEOFFREY. She's dotty. I don't see why, for the purpose of this exercise, your mother should come down here at all.

DEIRDRE. Darling, if we leave her up there in the house for three weeks on her own, anything could happen to her.

GEOFFREY. The 'daily' pops in from time to time.

DEIRDRE. An elderly lady, in mother's condition could go in the night.

GEOFFREY. My God, supposing she pops off down here? Very jolly.

DEIRDRE.. Well if she does, which God forbid, we'll just have to call this off and make the funeral arrangements.

GEOFFREY. But the whole point of this exercise is to make it as near the real thing as possible. Now, in the middle of the Third World War with three feet of radioactive dust covering the garden, and most of Northolt, one doesn't open the hatch to try and dispose of your mother!

DEIRDRE. But Geoffrey, if it was the real thing, what would we do with her?

GEOFFREY. I suppose we'd have to put her in the deep freeze here.

DEIRDRE. But that's all our rations in there, if we take them out they'll go off.

GEOFFREY. But not as quickly as your mother.

DEIRDRE. I don't think you've thought this thing through properly. Just tell me what we would do if you kicked the bucket.

GEOFFREY. Well you couldn't use the deep freeze for reasons already mentioned. Ah but wait — there is another solution. At the end of this pipe, behind that cupboard, there is a metal door, which opens inwards — now once you've opened this door you can dig your way into the garden.

DEIRDRE. What do I dig with?

GEOFFREY. Good thinking Deirdre — must bring a shovel down. Anyway you dig about six feet or thereabouts into that bank or in the case of your mother, five foot-three.

(MRS. WAYNEFLETE rattles her stick at the top of the stairs.)

Mrs. W. *(off)* Deirdre, are you there?

Deirdre. Yes mother.

Mrs. W. I'm coming down. *(DEIRDRE goes into the hall followed by GEOFFREY.)*

Deirdre. No, wait, you could hurt yourself, it's a very tricky staircase.

Mrs. W. *(Calls down.)* I'll be all right, as long as the sea remains calm. *(GEOFFREY & DEIRDRE look at each other.)*

Geoffrey. *(puzzled)* "The sea remains calm?" What in heaven's name have you told her?

Deirdre. I didn't want to upset her. You can't tell a seventy-year-old woman you're planning for Armageddon, so I said we were going on a little holiday.

Geoffrey. To the bottom of the garden?

Deirdre. I didn't specify anywhere in particular.

Mrs. W. Steward!

Geoffrey. She thinks she's on a cruise, dear.

Deirdre. As long as she's happy.

(MRS. W. reaches the hall. She is elderly, autocratic, dominating with odd moments of sanity, but this isn't one of them. She comes down the stairs with a parasol & a holdall.)

Mrs. W. I didn't see them putting my trunk on board.

Deirdre. No mother dear, I've brought down your things, you'll find them in your bedroom, under your bunk.

Mrs. W. Bunk? I want a cabin on the port side.

Geoffrey. Certainly. Welcome aboard, Madam, I'm

the Purser.

MRS. W. Geoffrey, why do you behave like a buffoon all the time?

GEOFFREY. Just a little joke, Mother.

DEIRDRE. This way, Mother.

GEOFFREY. Let me take that. *(He takes her holdall.)*

DEIRDRE. Come and sit down, Mother. *(Leads her into recreation room.)*

MRS. W. *(looking around)* I suppose it'll be all right, but it's one of the smallest boats I've ever been on, not Japanese is it?

GEOFFREY. No Mother, British through and through.

MRS. W. Oh, how very comforting.

DEIRDRE. You didn't have to come aboard yet, I'd've fetched you when it was time.

MRS. W. I had a terrible dream last night that you'd sailed away without me.

DEIRDRE. *(Puts an arm around her.)* I'd never do that.

MRS. W. No, but he would.

GEOFFREY. *(Ignores her.)* I'm just going up top. Still got one or two things to bring down.

DEIRDRE. If you see that phone man, tell him to hurry up.

GEOFFREY. Yes, will do. *(He rushes up the staircase.)*

MRS. W. I brought *The Forsyte Saga* with me, I always enjoy that.

DEIRDRE. I know you do, Mummy.

MRS. W. The world was so civilised and elegant in those days. I know one shouldn't live in the past, but then the past was so much more attractive to live in.

DEIRDRE. We do try to make the present as bearable for

you as possible, Mummy. We've got all your favourite things here, food, drink and entertainment.

MRS. W. Really?

DEIRDRE. Yes.

MRS. W. Video tapes?

DEIRDRE. Of course, and your favourite one of all — "Mrs Miniver."

MRS. W. Oh Greer Garson, she was so good. I can see I'm going to enjoy myself after all.

DEIRDRE. There, you see, I knew you would.

MRS. W. It's just that one doesn't meet one's own type of person on a package holiday, er, have you met any of the others?

DEIRDRE. No Mummy, there aren't any others, it's just us.

MRS. W. (reaching for her holdall & producing a book) Oh good, I think I'll settle down and have a little read.

(GRINDLE appears.)

GRINDLE. I think the baby does not want to sleep.

DEIRDRE. Babies are so sensitive to new surroundings. I'll see if I can get him off. (DEIRDRE exits into bedroom. GRINDLE makes to follow but is stopped by MRS.W.)

MRS. W. Are you looking forward to the cruise?

GRINDLE. Cruise?

MRS. W. On this boat.

GRINDLE. Oh yes, very much.

MRS. W. What is our first port of call?

GRINDLE. I think it's Rotterdam.

MRS. W. And then?

GRINDLE. Casablanca.

MRS. W. Casablanca? Surely we're not missing out Tangiers.

GRINDLE. You want to go to Tangiers?

MRS. W. Tangiers? Why certainly, the Bazaar there can be most rewarding. I bought a very nice Jellabi there 35 years ago.

GRINDLE. All right, we'll go.

MRS. W. I'm glad we're going back because unfortunately, it shrank and I'd like to have a word with them.

GRINDLE. Would you like a cup of coffee, or something?

MRS. W. No, no, no. I'll wait, then perhaps I'll take a beef tea on the main deck.

GRINDLE. I'll see you later, Mrs Wayneflete. *(GRINDLE leaves the recreation room as JOE appears down the stairs, he carries a canvas bag, a green phone & is paying out a roll of cable behind him.)*

GRINDLE. *(Crosses into kitchen. To JOE.)* I'm just going to make some coffee, would you like one? *(She switches on electric kettle.)*

JOE. That's very kind of you, darling. I'd be very grateful for anything you've got going. *(Follows her into kitchen.)* How long have you been over here, darling?

GRINDLE. Three months.

JOE. You've picked up the lingo toute suite.

GRINDLE. What?

JOE. You learned our language very quickly.

GRINDLE. Oh, I could speak before I came. I learned at school.

Joe. You must have better schools than what we got. I still have trouble with English.

Grindle. Yes, my ears tell me this.

Joe. And what do your eyes tell you? *(JOE looks very macho.)*

Grindle. That you would like to kiss me.

Joe. *(thrown)* Oh, well I wasn't going to come on that strong, that quick.

Grindle. I think it is good when you want to do something that you should do it.

Joe. Well I can't just do it like that.

Grindle. Why?

Joe. Because you make it sound about as exciting as licking a stamp. *(Looks around anxiously.)* Apart from which there are people about.

Grindle. Only Mrs. Wayneflete, and she wouldn't notice anything.

Joe. If it's all right with you I'll just settle for the coffee.

Grindle. White with sugar?

Joe. Yes, that's right. *(to himself)* I'll have the sauna and massage later. *(JOE takes his bag into recreation room where MRS. W. is reading. He goes to the junction box.)*

Mrs. W. Who are you?

Joe. I'm the engineer.

Mrs. W. Ah, of course, I should have known.

Joe. I'm putting it in for Mrs. Green. I mean Jones, she wanted green.

Mrs. W. What?

Joe. She wanted green.

Mrs. W. I heard that bit, what was the first bit?

JOE. I'm putting this phone in for Mrs. Jones.

MRS. W. That's my daughter.

JOE. Very nice lady.

MRS. W. Thank you.

JOE. Are you joining them for the duration?

MRS. W. Of course.

JOE. Rather you than me.

MRS. W. At my time of life three weeks seems very little. When you're young of course it could be an eternity.

JOE. It's the boredom that would get me. See I'm very active, I'd miss the football and the Pub.

MRS. W. We have plenty to pass the time, we have music, films and books.

JOE. You sound as if you're quite looking forward to it.

MRS. W. I am, and do you know it'll be the first time in 35 years that I've stepped ashore at Tangiers?

JOE. *(reacts)* Hang on a minute. What did they tell you you were on?

MRS. W. It's a winter cruise.

JOE. I see, and where's it going to?

MRS. W. Well you ought to know, if you're the engineer.

JOE. Excuse me. *(JOE goes into the hall & picks up the reel of cable, He calls to GRINDLE.)* I've changed my mind, strong black and no sugar. *(He returns to the job.)*

MRS. W. What are you doing down there?

JOE. Fixing the phone, Madam. This cable here is connected to the junction box outside.

MRS. W. Would you mind if I made an observation?

JOE. Feel free.

MRS. W. As soon as we cast off that'll snap.

JOE. Yes, I daresay it would.

MRS. W. Well, don't say I didn't warn you.

JOE. No Madam. As a matter of interest, what are you — er — er — aiming to do in Tangiers?

MRS. W. Go straight to the Bazaar and change my Jellabi.

JOE. Well, that would be a natural thing to do, wouldn't it.

(DEIRDRE enters.)

DEIRDRE. Thank goodness I've got him to sleep at last. Ah, that's just the colour I wanted. It tones in very nicely.

JOE. I'm relieved about that as it's the only green we've got.

DEIRDRE. May I suggest you ask your people to delay the bill for 3 weeks, otherwise it'll just lie on the mat unpaid, and we wouldn't like to be cut off.

JOE. Well you can always get out at Gibralter and pop a cheque in the post.

DEIRDRE. Gibralter?

JOE. Or Tangiers. Of course you could get lucky, I mean if they press the button in Moscow you won't have to pay at all.

MRS. W. I didn't know we were going to Moscow.

DEIRDRE. We're not, Mother.

MRS. W. It'll be freezing and I've only got summer clothes.

JOE. Don't worry, we're cruising around in the Med.

MRS. W. You didn't know where we were going just now.

JOE. Well down in the engine room — stripped to the waist, shovelling coal, sweat pouring off us, we got no clue where we're going. It's *(sings)*
TOTE THAT BARGE, LIFT THAT BALE,
GET A LITTLE DRUNK AND YOU LAND IN
    GAOL.........

DEIRDRE. *(interrupting)* I gather you've had a chat with Mother.

JOE. Yes, we touched lightly on the trip ahead.

DEIRDRE. Mother, you are a chatterbox.

MRS. W. I never think it does any harm to be friendly with the crew.

JOE. Excuse me, I'm just going to make a test call to the Bridge. *(Dials number.)*

DEIRDRE. Ask them how they'd like us to pay the bill.

JOE. That's "Accounts." *(into phone)* Mr. Bearstead? Joe here, just testing the connection on Docket no. 12, 5, 4, 3, 2, 1. Alpha, Beta, Gamma, Delta. Mary had a little lamb, the doctor was surprised — over — *(He pauses & listens.)* Your response is clear.

MRS. W. Ask him what the weather forecast is.

JOE. Eh?

MRS. W. You're through to the Bridge, aren't you?

JOE. Oh yes — it's the Captain himself.

MRS. W. Well, go on, ask him.

JOE. *(into phone)* Lady down here wants to know about

the weather.... I see, *(Puts phone down.)* Portland Bill, Ronaldsway and Rockall — ten degrees falling. Visibility clear to moderate on the Western Avenue. *(He winks at DEIRDRE.)*

MRS. W. That sounds hopeful.

DEIRDRE. I should get on with your book, dear.

MRS. W. It would be nice to have some music. Perhaps a little Mantovani.

DEIRDRE. We haven't unpacked yet.

MRS. W. Let me know when we're going to cast off — I always like to wave goodbye to England.

DEIRDRE. I will, dear.

JOE. I only wish I could hang around, I wouldn't mind seeing that myself. *(During the above, GRINDLE has made a coffee & is seated reading a magazine in the kitchen.)*

DEIRDRE. *(to JOE)* Well, thank you very much for being so obliging.

JOE. All part of the service.

DEIRDRE. *(Starts up the stairs, then feeling insecure, she turns & comes down again.)* After you.

JOE. As a matter of fact, a very attractive lady offered me a coffee a while back.

DEIRDRE. *(flattered)* Oh, I don't remember doing that.

JOE. Not you, darling, the Nordic Nanny.

DEIRDRE. Well, I've got one or two last minute things to see to up top.

JOE. Be my guest.

DEIRDRE. *(Walks cautiously up the stairs, then stops & turns.)* These stairs are very awkward.

JOE. Mind how you go then.

DEIRDRE. Why don't you go and have your coffee?

JOE. I want to be here to catch you in my arms in case you fall.

DEIRDRE. I shan't fall, I'm in no danger of falling. *(She goes up the stairs.)*

GRINDLE. I still have it hot if you want it.

JOE. Spoilt for choice. *(Goes into kitchen. GRINDLE takes saucer off a cup of coffee for JOE. He sits down at table.)* Ta. Are you going to be able to stand this?

GRINDLE. What?

JOE. Being trapped down here with a family of lunatics.

GRINDLE. The Jones are very nice people. I am very happy with them.

JOE. When you're free to walk out on them, yes, but not encased in steel, 25 feet under the garden, it's a bit macabre isn't it?

GRINDLE. What?

JOE. Weird. Living down here. I mean it's creepy.

GRINDLE. It would not be very pleasant to be dying of radiation.

JOE. Nobody's going to die, if they've got the bomb and we've got the bomb nobody's going to use it.

GRINDLE. If, like me, you'd come from near Eastern Europe, you would not feel so safe.

JOE. Well you're not in Eastern Europe now, dear, you're in Northolt.

GRINDLE. And I shall tell you why I'm in Northolt. The main reason I took this job is because they advertised — "Own room, T.V. and atomic bomb shelter."

JOE. I don't believe this. How can people get so

hysterical.

GRINDLE. I am not hysterical, do I look hysterical?

JOE. Maybe not yet, but once that door shuts you'll be halfway to claustrophobism, I mean you won't see daylight for 3 weeks. God, how can you take it all so calmly?

GRINDLE. I have my books and plenty of music.

JOE. Mantovani? You call that music? I'd go crazy, I'd go bananas.

MRS. W. *(calling)* I'll have my beef tea now.

JOE. Oh God, imagine what it could do to her. I mean she's got a headstart on everybody already.

(GEOFFREY appears at the top of the stairs with a set of golf clubs.)

GEOFFREY. Anyone around to give me a hand?

JOE. I'm still here, what is it?

GEOFFREY. Rather heavy, golf clubs.

JOE. *(to GRINDLE)* Golf clubs, you still telling me they're sane?

GRINDLE. *(Goes into hall.)* Can I help you Mr. Jones?

GEOFFREY. It's all right, Grindle, I'll just put them here for now. *(GRINDLE returns to kitchen.)*

JOE. By my reckoning this whole pipe is about forty feet from end to end. I should hardly think you'd need a set of irons just for a long putt.

GEOFFREY. No, you see they're brand new.

JOE. Gold or platinum?

GEOFFREY. Being metal, they would retain radioactive properties for years to come, if they are exposed to a nuclear explosion. That, of course, is if they hadn't already melted in the blast.

JOE. You take this whole thing very seriously don't you?

GEOFFREY. One has to treat this operation in the firm belief that it could happen.

JOE. I can see it now. It's finally happened — Wham!! Two or three months go by while the dust settles. Then one bright morning a smartly dressed figure steps onto the first tee at Northolt Golf Club and shouts — "If there's anyone left in the world, 'fore.' "

MRS. W. *(Calls out.)* Have we cast off?

GEOFFREY. No mother. *(Calls out.)* All ashore those who are going ashore.

JOE. While we're waiting for the big bang, I'll settle for a pint in the local until someone calls out "Time" in that great pub in the sky. *(He starts up the stairs.)*

GEOFFREY. *(stopping him)* Mr. Parker, it's people like you who make light of the future of Britain.

JOE. And because people like me can't afford one of your de-luxe shelters, all that's going to be left of Britain is twits like you. *(Exits up the stairs.)*

GEOFFREY. *(to himself)* Thank you very much. I'm rather glad he didn't vote for me.

GRINDLE. *(Comes out of the kitchen with a cup of Bovril.)* Would you like a cup of something hot Mr. Jones?

GEOFFREY. No thank you, Grindle, I think I could do with something a little stronger.

GRINDLE. A whisky maybe?

GEOFFREY. Yes.

GRINDLE. I will get it for you when I've given this to

Mrs. Wayneflete.

GEOFFREY. Quite all right, I'll do it myself.

MRS. W. I'm still waiting.

GRINDLE. Coming. *(GRINDLE goes into recreation room. GEOFFREY goes into kitchen.)* Here we are Mrs. Wayneflete, a nice hot cup of beef tea.

> MRS. W. Thank you, my dear. *(GEOFFREY is getting ice from the fridge & refilling the ice trays.)*

(The baby cries.)

> MRS. W. *(irritated)* I hope we shan't have too much of that. If he's like that now, what's he going to be like crossing the Bay of Biscay?

GRINDLE. I think the motion of the ship will lull him to sleep.

MRS. W. I hope so. That can ruin a cruise. Go in and give him a comforter, or a rusk, or something.

GRINDLE. OK, Mrs. Wayneflete. *(She exits to bedroom. The baby stops crying.)*

GEOFFREY. *(Puts the ice trays in the fridge, dries his hands & looks at his watch.)* I think there's just time for a quick one. *(He presses a button on the wall above the sink & bar door opens. It is as vast as possible and stocked from floor to ceiling like a wine cellar. He goes into the bar.)*

(DEIRDRE comes down the stairs with a bunch of cut daffodils and some letters.)

> DEIRDRE. *(calling)* Grindle .... Grindle dear.

MRS. W. She's in with that baby.

DEIRDRE. Oh. I just wanted her to put these in water. Never mind, I'll do it myself. *(She goes into kitchen & sees GEOFFREY in the bar.)* Starting a little early aren't we, dear?

GEOFFREY. Just making sure that it's all in working order.

DEIRDRE. The second post's arrived.

GEOFFREY. Read it later, give us something to do. Care to join me in a snifter, darling?

DEIRDRE. Oh well, all right. *(Looks in.)* What have you got?

GEOFFREY. Well, if you've got an hour to spare, I'll tell you.

DEIRDRE. I think just a little gin, dear.

GEOFFREY. Can do. Pink? Tonic? Bitter lemon? Lime? Orange?

DEIRDRE. Yes.

GEOFFREY. Yes what?

DEIRDRE. Whatever you said — I don't mind, surprise me. *(She takes the daffodils to sink.)*

GEOFFREY. What are you doing with those flowers?

DEIRDRE. I'm just going to put them in water. *(She turns on the tap.)*

GEOFFREY. *(Ducks hurriedly under the flap with his whisky & turns the tap off.)* Lesson one. Water is our most precious commodity, our life blood, without it we perish and we only have two and a half thousand gallons. Now that has to last 5 people probably for as many months. We can only use it for things that are absolutely essential. *(He casually turns on the tap to top up his whisky.)* Flowers are out, I can't think why you brought them down. They are lethal in an enclosed space. Even as I speak those flowers are using up the air in the room.

DEIRDRE. Well I didn't want to leave them in the garden for the neighbours to pinch.

GEOFFREY. The Blakes? Do you think they'd do that?

DEIRDRE. I'm sure of it. When we went on our Spring Holiday last year they ravaged the daffodils.

GEOFFREY. You can't prove that.

DEIRDRE. I don't know why they don't plant some themselves, they have copied everything else we've got.

GEOFFREY. Have they?

DEIRDRE. Of course. Haven't you noticed?

GEOFFREY. Not particularly.

DEIRDRE. We get a barbecue — they get a barbecue. We get a Flymo — they get one. We go over to Gas Central Heating, and a week later they've got it. I didn't realize there was so much money in the scrap metal business.

GEOFFREY. He also makes dodgy videos.

DEIRDRE. Dodgy?

GEOFFREY. "X" certificate stuff.

DEIRDRE. That's only a rumour, dear.

GEOFFREY. No, a chap at the Golf Club told me he'd seen one, starring Mrs. Blake.

DEIRDRE. No.

GEOFFREY. Yes.

DEIRDRE. Did she have a big part?

GEOFFREY. Apparently enormous.

DEIRDRE. Thay don't quite fit into Oswald Crescent.

GEOFFREY. No. I knew what we were in for when they changed the name of their house from Mandalay to Cobblers.

DEIRDRE. What's wrong with Cobblers? It's rather quaint, it has an old-world ring to it.

GEOFFREY. Think about it, darling, he's in Pornography!

DEIRDRE. What. Cobblers? .... Of course, I hadn't put the two together.

GEOFFREY. Here's your drink, darling.

DEIRDRE. Cheers!!

(A pair of black-trousered legs appear on the staircase & a voice calls out.)

VOICE. Can I have a word with you, Mrs. Jones?

GEOFFREY. Who's that?

DEIRDRE. It's only the milkman. *(She goes into hall.)* What is it milkman?

VOICE. I got your note stopping the milk but you haven't paid the bill.

DEIRDRE. I'm not sure where my bag is.

(An Indian milkman, CLIVE PATEL comes down the stairs wearing Express Dairy uniform & a peaked cap.)

PATEL. So this is the day of days, Mr. Jones, three weeks isn't it you're going to be down here?

GEOFFREY. How did you work that out?

PATEL. *(Produces note.)* Because on this note it says "two

pints and a dozen eggs on the fourteenth."

GEOFFREY. I'm surprised you didn't put a notice up on the window, Deirdre, — "Jones's gone to ground for 3 weeks."

DEIRDRE. Darling, the milkman saw it being built, you can hardly keep it a secret for a month, with an earth mover and a crane in the drive.

PATEL. I will never forget the morning I saw this whole edifice hoisted in the air, it blotted out the sun like a huge galactic chariot, then down it sank deep into the bowels of the earth, like a dead whale.

GEOFFREY. You could have chosen a slightly cheerier simile.

PATEL. Ah forgive me, Mr. Jones. That is what I am thinking before I am coming down these stairs and seeing this most desirable maisonette.

GEOFFREY. Well I wouldn't quarrel with that description — Mr. er — er—

PATEL. Patel. Clive Patel.

GEOFFREY. Mr. Patel. It has all mod. cons. and sophisticated electric controls for oxygen, cooking, refridgeration and sleeps six in comfort.

PATEL. Would I be rising above my station if I ask the price of all this?

GEOFFREY. Not at all, there are cheaper versions than this, but what you are standing in now costs around fifteen thousand pounds.

PATEL. Well, I'll go to the foot of Anaratapura. I can hardly believe it. To think that I paid twice that for a rat-infested leaking hovel, on the Waverley Estate.

DEIRDRE. Oh come along now, Mr. Patel, they're not

that bad.

PATEL. I felt safer when I was flooded out every year on the Ganges.

GEOFFREY. Steady on, there's a little thing known as slander, my firm designed that estate and if the people on it have let it go to rack and ruin that's not our fault.

PATEL. Well, I'm telling you this. If you could sell my house again and get me one of these I would be a very happy man.

GEOFFREY. Come on, Mr. Patel, would you really fancy living underground?

PATEL. If it is the difference of living underground and dying above it, it is the only sensible thing to do.

DEIRDRE. Do you mean you're one of the few people who believe that we're in danger of being annihilated?

PATEL. I feel it with a deep certainty. The Russians are in Afghanistan, the only logical reason for their presence is that they are going to sweep down through India like a bush fire.

GEOFFREY. What would they want India for?

PATEL. Seven hundred million people ripe for conquering and conversion. That's not counting the one's in Hounslow.

DEIRDRE. I can't see the Indians fighting for the Russians.

PATEL. Why not? There is a very good precedent, you conquered us and we fought for you. Why else would I be speaking a ruddy difficult language like English and working for the Express Dairy company?

GEOFFREY. Hadn't thought of it like that. We're indebted to you.

PATEL. And you to me, eight pounds, thirty-five.

DEIRDRE. Have you got any money, darling?

GEOFFREY. I've already given you the house-keeping.

DEIRDRE. Oh yes. I'll just see if my bag's in the bed-room. *(She goes to bedroom.)*

GEOFFREY. Won't keep you a jiffy, Mr. Patel.

PATEL. That's quite all right. I've almost finished my round.

GEOFFREY. Short day eh? Not a bad life.

PATEL. I was up at four, Mr. Jones.

GEOFFREY. Ah.

PATEL. And I will be working until nine o'clock tonight in my brother's supermarket in Hounslow.

GEOFFREY. God, you must be rolling in it. What are you doing with all the money?

PATEL. Underpinning my house. *(DEIRDRE comes back into recreation room from bedroom.)*

GEOFFREY. *(calls)* Got your bag yet, dear?

DEIRDRE. No, darling.

GEOFFREY. Mr. Patel wants to go.

DEIRDRE. *(to MRS. W.)* Mother, Mother, dear.

MRS. W. *(Wakes up.)* What is it?

DEIRDRE. Your bag, dear, I want to borrow some money.

MRS. W. Have we cast off yet?

DEIRDRE. No. *(Takes Mrs. W's bag.)*

MRS. W. You will let me know won't you? Because I want to be on deck when we pass the Isle of Wight.

PATEL. *(overhearing)* Pass the Isle of Wight. What? What? *(to GEOFFREY)* Pass the Isle of Wight?

GEOFFREY. Um — it's my mother-in-law, she's not

entirely with us at the moment. She thinks she's on a cruise.

PATEL. Well it is good to revere the aged. You are not seeing that often in this country.

GEOFFREY. Well, we're not the sort to leave her up there to perish in the blast.

DEIRDRE. Thank you, Mother.

MRS. W. That beef tea's gone straight through me.

DEIRDRE. Well go to the bathroom, dear.

MRS. W. I haven't the faintest idea where it is.

DEIRDRE. I'll show you, Mother, it's this way.

MRS. W. Is it all right to use it while we're still in harbour?

DEIRDRE. Of course, dear.

GEOFFREY. It's beside the stairs, Mother.

MRS. W. *(seeing PATEL)* Oh good morning, Captain.

GEOFFREY. Here we go again.

MRS. W. Making your final rounds?

PATEL. Oh yes, this is definitely my final round.

MRS. W. I wonder if I could prevail on your kindness?

PATEL. Yes.

MRS. W. I would be honoured if I could sit at your table for dinner.

PATEL. *(somewhat thrown)* Oh. What? What?

GEOFFREY. The Captain hasn't made up his table yet.

PATEL. I haven't what?

GEOFFREY. I'm sure the Captain *(nudging PATEL)* the Captain will bear you in mind.

PATEL. Most certainly. See you at the second sitting.

DEIRDRE. *(to MRS. W.)* It's just around the corner, dear. Just press the button, it's an electric flush.

MRS. W. Thank you, it's not a banana boat is it?

DEIRDRE. No. Why?

MRS. W. *(in a loud whisper)* It's just that the Captain looks rather dark. *(She exits into bathroom.)*

GEOFFREY. God, that woman.

DEIRDRE. I'm awfully sorry, Mr. Patel.

PATEL. Don't apologise. I am quite flattered to be thought of as someone as elevated as a Captain of a banana boat.

GEOFFREY. *(changing the subject)* Thanks for popping down.

DEIRDRE. *(paying him)* Here's your money, Mr. Patel.

PATEL. Ah. Thank you. *(He takes two fivers.)* Here is your change. Thirty five, forty, fifty, nine pounds and a picture of the Queen.

GEOFFREY. See you again in 3 weeks.

PATEL. God willing. I know this is only a trial run you are having but if things do get worse, and war breaks out, would it be all right if I came and knocked on your door for shelter?

GEOFFREY. Ah yes — well the point is, you see, if it does come to the crunch we'll have a lot of relatives, close relatives, billetting themselves on us. Isn't that so, Deirdre?

DEIRDRE. Yes, there's my aunt in Folkestone.

GEOFFREY. And I've got a very close cousin in — er — where does whatsis-name live?

DEIRDRE. Cornwall.

GEOFFREY. Yes — Cornwall.

PATEL. After the four-minute warning goes, your cousin could be very short of breath by the time he reaches this shelter.

GEOFFREY. We also have people nearer.

DEIRDRE. Were it not for all these close relatives you would, of course, be more than welcome.

PATEL. Well it's the thought that counts.

GEOFFREY. Can you let yourself out?

PATEL. *(Goes to the foot of the stairs & trips on the bottom one.)* I hope if the bomb comes, you will be able to climb quickly up this very awkward staircase to shut the door.

GEOFFREY. No problem. All we have to do is pull this lever here and half a ton of metal slams down and locks itself into position.

PATEL. Oh, you have thought of everything, Mr. Jones.

GEOFFREY. Well we hope so, and if we haven't we'll know more about it at the end of 3 weeks time.

(The lights go down & then slowly up & then down again & up.)

DEIRDRE. What's happening?

GEOFFREY. It's that damn flush, it's shorting the circuit.

(The lights go down.)

GEOFFREY. *(Goes to the door & bangs on it.)* Mother! Stop pushing that button.

(The lights come up, then go down & up very quickly.)

DEIRDRE. You'd better check this, Geoffrey. I mean this is just one cup of beef tea.

PATEL. At this rate, one dodgy curry and you could all be living in the dark.

(JOE comes down the stairs.)

JOE. Ah, I'm glad I caught you before you closed.

GEOFFREY. Only just.

JOE. I left my bag of equipment in there.

GEOFFREY. Good job you remembered, or you'd'd've been without it for 3 weeks. *(Exits into kitchen for the bag.)*

JOE. *(eyeing PATEL)* 'Ere don't you live on the Waverley Estate?

PATEL. If you can call it living.

JOE. Thought so, corner of Kenilworth and Talisman?

PATEL. That's right.

JOE. I'm just up the road from you, number 18.

PATEL. Well goodness me, what a small world.

GEOFFREY. *(Comes out of kitchen with JOE's tool bag.)* Quite a weight, what've you got in there?

JOE. A vandalised telephone call box. *(He takes his bag.)*

DEIRDRE. I wonder there are any left.

JOE. So long all.

GEOFFREY. Goodbye.

DEIRDRE. Goodbye.

JOE. *(Starts up the stairs, stops suddenly & comes back down.)* Oh sorry, I forgot to get you to sign for the installation.

GEOFFREY. Oh, all right, have you got a pen?

JOE. Oh yes. *(He casually hangs his tool bag on the lever which has a large red knob on the end.)*

(The lever slowly tilts down & as it comes to a stop there is a metallic clang as the hatch slams shut, thereby shutting out the shaft of sunlight & cutting the telephone cable which drops to the floor. They all look up & then towards each other.)

GEOFFREY. Your bag did that.

JOE. Sorry Squire. *(He removes his bag from the lever.)*

PATEL. Well we know it works.

DEIRDRE. At least we won't hear the bomb, dear, we'll all be deaf.

PATEL. Pardon?

GEOFFREY. *(Grasps the lever.)* Just open it and let off the visitors and then we'll weigh anchor.

DEIRDRE. Geoffrey please! You're sounding like Mother.

GEOFFREY. *(heaving on the immovable lever)* It's stuck, it's stuck!

DEIRDRE. Oh don't be ridiculous.

JOE. It better not be. *(He grabs it along side GEOFFREY.)* Come on push!

GEOFFREY. I am pushing!

DEIRDRE. Help them, Milkman.

PATEL. Yes, Madam.

Joe. Come on. *(All three men strain with grunts & groans to push the lever up, but instead it snaps off in GEOFFREY's hands.)*

Geoffrey. My God.

Deirdre. What's happened?

Patel. Bloody British workmanship. That is what's happened!

CURTAIN

ACT ONE
Scene Two

The same. The action is continuous. JOE & GEOFFREY have run
up the stairs. JOE is banging loudly on the hatch with the
broken lever. DEIRDRE & PATEL are at the foot of the
stairs. PATEL grabs GEOFFREY's driver from the golf bag
& bangs it on the hand rail of the stairs.

PATEL. Help! Help!
GEOFFREY. Have you gone mad?
PATEL. No but I am on the way.
GEOFFREY. Give me that club.
PATEL. Why?
GEOFFREY. You're not even holding it properly. *(GEOF-*
FREY grabs it from PATEL, and puts it back in the bag.)

(GRINDLE enters from the bedroom & runs into hall.)

GRINDLE. The baby cannot sleep with such a terrible noise.
GEOFFREY. *(shouting)* Half a dozen sticks of dynamite
couldn't open that hatch.
JOE. I'm not trying to open it, I'm trying to attract
attention.
GEOFFREY. Whose attention?

JOE. Passers by.

GEOFFREY. Strange as it may seem, we get very few passers by strolling through our back garden.

GRINDLE. Is something the matter?

DEIRDRE. Just a hitch — my husband is dealing with it.

GEOFFREY. There's not a damn thing your husband can do.

JOE. *(Comes down the stairs looking dejected and holding the lever.)* Well, this is very jolly, isn't it?

PATEL. How can you be so calm? *(Fans himself with his cap.)* I am already having the claustrophobia.

GEOFFREY. Absolute nonsense, Patel, it's all in the mind.

DEIRDRE. Well where else would it be, you fool. *(to PATEL)* Now it's all right, Mr. Patel, come along with me.

PATEL. Thank you, thank you.

DEIRDRE. Come and sit down. *(He does.)* Just relax and take a few deep breaths. *(PATEL sits gasping.)* Mr. Patel, relax.

PATEL. How can I relax when my brain is telling me that we are trapped like rats in a sewer?

GEOFFREY. That's absolute rubbish.

PATEL. But you've just said there's not a damn thing you can do.

GEOFFREY. How can I think clearly with you having hysterics?

PATEL. I tell you we are doomed to die.

GEOFFREY. *(Puts PATEL's cap firmly on PATEL's head.)* **Pull yourself together man, and remember you belong to the**

Express Dairy Company.

PATEL. *(calmly)* Yes, I'm sorry, but this is the first time in my ten years as a Roundsman that I have been trapped 25 feet beneath a customer's back garden.

DEIRDRE. I think we'd all feel better if we had a nice cup of tea.

(The lights dim & go up again.)

GEOFFREY. Not beef tea.

DEIRDRE. Grindle, tea please.

GRINDLE. Does everyone take milk and sugar?

JOE. You can put some brandy in mine, girl.

(MRS. WAYNEFLETE enters from bathroom.)

MRS. W. I heard a bang, does that mean we're at sea?

DEIRDRE. Very much so, Mother. *(to GEOFFREY)* Darling, you implied earlier that you'd covered every eventuality.

GEOFFREY. All bar one.

JOE. The 'andle coming off in your hand.

GEOFFREY. Exactly.

DEIRDRE. Why can't you phone for another one?

GEOFFREY. Of course, I knew I couldn't have been that stupid, that's why I had the phone put in.

JOE. *(Holds up the severed end of the cable.)* Where d'you want me to put the end of the cable, in your ear, or in your mouth?

GEOFFREY. What happened?

JOE. Cut off by the door.

MRS. W. I warned you that would happen. *(She walks into the living room & resumes reading her book.)*

DEIRDRE. Didn't you see that piece of conduit piping this was supposed to run through?

JOE. Did you ask me to look for it?

GEOFFREY. I wasn't here when you ran the cable in.

JOE. Well I'm not clairvoyant.

GEOFFREY. Didn't you tell him, Deirdre?

DEIRDRE. Don't be stupid, darling, of course I didn't. That's your department.

GEOFFREY. Yes, I forgot you were probably doing something terribly vital, like the flowers.

DEIRDRE. Do you think we could have this acrimonious conversation without the tradesmen present?

JOE. Don't mind us, darling, we quite enjoy seeing a bit of middle-class mud fly.

GEOFFREY. Mr. Parker, we are not going to improve matters if we start insulting each other and please don't refer to Mrs. Jones as a "darling."

DEIRDRE. I can't see it matters what the hell he calls me, when we're stuck down here in this bloody contraption of yours.

GEOFFREY. It's not forever, it's only a temporary hiccup.

PATEL. How do you know it's only temporary?

GEOFFREY. Because in 3 weeks time, my office manager, Jerry Hanssen, is getting married.

PATEL. I fail to see the connection between your office manager's wedding and our present predicament.

GEOFFREY. Because I'm Jerry Hanssen's best man, and

when I don't show up for the stag party at the Eve Club, he'll come and look for me.

DEIRDRE. You never mentioned a stag party.

GEOFFREY. Didn't I?

DEIRDRE. And certainly not at the Eve Club, that's a strip place, isn't it?

GEOFFREY. Only the top part.

DEIRDRE. What?

GEOFFREY. I mean upstairs.

DEIRDRE. Well you're the best man, you must've arranged it.

GEOFFREY. Could we forget the stag party, it's not of paramount importance and it's not for 3 weeks.

JOE. They're bound to miss you in the House of Commons.

DEIRDRE. I doubt it, he's never caught the Speaker's eye yet.

GEOFFREY. It happens to be the summer recess.

PATEL. Three weeks, we could all be dead by then.

GEOFFREY. Don't be silly, Patel, we've got plenty of oxygen, food and water. All the equipment here is still under guarantee. I have complete confidence in its efficiency.

PATEL. I wish I could share your confidence, already you have broken the escape handle, and one cup of beef tea has buggered the lavatory.

DEIRDRE. My mother's here, Patel, and I'd rather she didn't hear that sort of language.

JOE. Could I interrupt just to say how glad I am that you've got a lavatory because I'd like to go for a gypsy's.

DEIRDRE. I beg your pardon?

JOE. Point Percy at the porcelain.

DEIRDRE. *(mystified)* I'm sorry?

JOE. How do you want me to put it without offending the old lady?

GEOFFREY. It's beside the stairs and be careful how you press the button.

JOE. Ta. *(exits)*

DEIRDRE. Who's Percy, darling?

GEOFFREY. Never mind, Deirdre.

PATEL. Why did I do it, I ask myself, why did I do it?

GEOFFREY. Do what?

PATEL. If it hadn't been for the money, a mere eight pounds, thirty five pence, I could still be up there in the sunlight, breathing the fresh air of Northolt.

GEOFFREY. *(Snaps fingers.)* Of course! Why didn't I think of it, we shall be out of here in no time.

DEIRDRE. Oh thank God darling, how?

GEOFFREY. Because when our friend, Mr. Patel, fails to return to the Depot, the Express Dairy Company will send out a search party.

DEIRDRE. How will they know where he is?

GEOFFREY. Because they'll see his little electric cart outside our gate — ergo Patel must still be in the vicinity: small search party, rooting around garden, hear faint sounds of banging on hatch, summon police, explosive expert called in, boom, boom, bang and we're out.

PATEL. I'm sorry to disappoint you, Mr. Jones, but they'll simply assume I've absconded with the week's takings.

GEOFFREY. Oh, yes, so they will..........

DEIRDRE. What about your wife when you don't arrive home?

PATEL. She's gone to Bombay for a holiday.

GEOFFREY. What about your brother you work for at the supermarket?

PATEL. He's gone to Bombay with my wife.

GEOFFREY. Well, one thing's certain. If we ever get out of here, I'm changing to Unigate.

PATEL. I'm sorry but I'm feeling a little unwell. Please don't mention Unigate to me.

DEIRDRE. Wait a minute, we've forgotten Joe.

GEOFFREY. Joe?

DEIRDRE. Surely British Telecom will come looking for him?

GEOFFREY. So they will! Where is he?

(The lights dim & go up again.)

GEOFFREY. Oh there he is........

GRINDLE. *(Starts to put the tea bags into the cups. To PATEL)* Do you take India tea?

PATEL. Haven't you got any of the Earl Grey?

GRINDLE. I don't think so.

GEOFFREY. You're damned lucky to get a cup of tea at all, without being choosy.

PATEL. I am sorry. *(GRINDLE pours hot water into each cup.)*

DEIRDRE. *(Pours milk into the cups.)* Make the most of this, it's the last of the real thing before we start the powdered stuff.

(JOE comes out of the bathroom & walks into kitchen during the following dialogue.)

GEOFFREY. *(looking at her)* It staggers me, it absolutely staggers me.

DEIRDRE. What does?

GEOFFREY. Tea can only come out of those little holes when it's submerged in boiling water.

DEIRDRE. I know that.

GEOFFREY. So why pour in cold milk before they've started working? That water's no longer boiling — ergo — no infusion!

DEIRDRE. What an extraordinary thing to lose your temper about!!

GEOFFREY. I realize now why I've been drinking tasteless brown water for the past ten years.

DEIRDRE. That's the last time I make a cup of tea for you.

GEOFFREY. Well as you've never actually succeeded it's hardly likely to affect me.

DEIRDRE. Oh you pig-headed idiot!!

JOE. *(going to her)* Now don't take on so, darling.

GEOFFREY. *(banging the table)* And DON'T call my wife darling.

JOE. I reckon someone should.

DEIRDRE. Thank you.

JOE. Don't mention it. *(He tears a piece of paper towel off & gives it to her.)* Dry your eyes on this.

PATEL. If it is any consolation to you, sir, this is exactly how I am liking my tea.

GEOFFREY. I don't give a stuff how you like it.

PATEL. It was merely an observation, sir.

JOE. Look, could we just cool it for a second, use a bit of self-control? Remember that submarine film, "We Dive at Dawn"?

GEOFFREY. What's that got to do with it?

JOE. Well, you didn't see John Mills hopping up and down complaining about the tea bags.

GEOFFREY. They didn't have tea bags in those days.

JOE. You're bloody impossible, you are. *(to DEIRDRE)* How do you live with him?

DEIRDRE. God knows.

JOE. *(putting his arm around her)* All right girl?

GEOFFREY. Will you please leave my wife alone?

DEIRDRE. Geoffrey, stop shouting!

GEOFFREY. *(shouting)* I'm not shouting!!

MRS. W. Is anything the matter?

DEIRDRE. No, Mother.

PATEL. We're just dying, that's all!!

GEOFFREY. *(loudly)* Stop being hysterical.

DEIRDRE. The pot calling the kettle black.

PATEL. I beg your pardon?

DEIRDRE. *(quickly)* No offence, Mr. Patel.

GEOFFREY. Mr. Parker, I suggest you go and wait in the hall until your people come for you.

JOE. My people?

GEOFFREY. Yes.

DEIRDRE. Who d'you think he is? Moses?

GEOFFREY. I mean British Telecom.

JOE. I shouldn't put money on it.

GEOFFREY. What d'you mean, they know you're here, don't they?

JOE. No.

GEOFFREY. But your van's outside.

JOE. No.

GEOFFREY. How did you get here?

JOE. On my motorbike. I delivered the van back to the depot and then remembered I'd left the tools here and came back for them on my way to Luton.

GEOFFREY. Well, when you don't report for your next job at Luton, they'll know you're missing.

PATEL. *(hopefully)* Yes, yes.

DEIRDRE. And perhaps track you back to here.

PATEL. Yes, yes.

JOE. No, no. I was going to Luton to catch a plane for Benidorm.

PATEL. *(dispairingly)* Oh then all hope is gone. *(Starts to pray on his knees.)* Hari Krishna, Hari Krishna.....

GEOFFREY. I'm not going to tell you again, Patel.

PATEL. I know. Express Dairy Company.

GRINDLE. Perhaps Mr. Parker's wife will report him missing?

DEIRDRE. He hasn't got a wife.

GEOFFREY. How do we know?

DEIRDRE. You don't know. He only told me!

GEOFFREY. Well surely he must be taking a girl with him to Benidorm?

JOE. No, I'm going on my own.

PATEL. Oh my God.

JOE. Well there's a lot of desperate crumpet out there.

GEOFFREY. So, to add to our troubles we're trapped down here with a sex maniac.

JOE. Jealously'll get you nowhere.

GEOFFREY. I don't think this is a very suitable subject to discuss in front of Grindle.

GRINDLE. We are quite used to free love in our country.

GEOFFREY. We don't happen to be in your country, Grindle. We're in England.

PATEL. We couldn't be more in England if we tried.

DEIRDRE. Well, if nobody is going to come to look for anybody, our only hope is Gerry Hanssen. Do you think he'll notice your absence at that strip club?

GEOFFREY. Well, he'll certainly notice the next day if I'm not standing beside him in top hat and morning coat, giving him the ring. So we must just accept that we're down here for 3 weeks and make the best of it. *(PATEL starts gasping for breath.)*

GRINDLE. How can you make the best of claustrophobia?

GEOFFREY. That won't last. He's perking up already. He's even a better colour.

DEIRDRE. *(reprovingly)* Darling, please.

GEOFFREY. Well, I can understand how he felt. I mean to say, we all had a momentary twinge, even me, and I've been under tremendous strain. Actually Parker was the first one to crack, he was up those stairs like a bolt out of the blue. But let's face it, it could have been any one of us.

GRINDLE. Would anyone like some more tea?

GEOFFREY. I think I'll have something a little stronger.

JOE. I never got my brandy, did I?

GEOFFREY. Would you like something?

JOE. Yes I would.

GEOFFREY. Light ale, shandy, cider, just name it.

JOE. I 'ave done. Brandy.

GEOFFREY. I see.

DEIRDRE. The gas bill, dear.

GEOFFREY. Well that can wait. *(to PATEL)* Would you care for a little something, Mr. Patel? To steady the nerves?

PATEL. I never drink, it is against my religion.

GEOFFREY. That's a bit of luck, don't you drink anything?

PATEL. Oh yes, milk.

DEIRDRE. *(reading from a letter)* Molly says — "are we going to join them in Frinton this year?"

GEOFFREY. *(forlornly)* Who knows?

GRINDLE. Now we are seven, we shall have to put two more bunks up.

GEOFFREY. Well there's room for one in the bathroom and one in the hall.

GRINDLE. Where would you like your bunk up Mr. Parker?

JOE. There's no answer to that.

DEIRDRE. *(reading third letter)* Oh God, no. I don't believe it.

GEOFFREY. What is it?

DEIRDRE. Darling. *(Hands GEOFFREY the letter.)*

PATEL. Somebody has died?

DEIRDRE. Far worse.

GEOFFREY. My God, it's Jerry Hanssen's wedding.

JOE. What about it?

GEOFFREY. It's been called off. *(There's a moment while the implications of this news sinks in, then one by one, with the exception of GRINDLE they make a dash for the stairs. JOE is first, followed by GEOFFREY, who picks up the broken lever & they both rush up & start beating the hatch cover for help. PATEL & DEIRDRE follow.)*

MRS. W. *(Rises and rings her handbell.)* What on earth's going on? Captain, Captain?

PATEL. Oh yes, Mrs. Wayneflete. *(Adjusts his tie and straightens cap.)*

MRS. W. I demand to know what is happening.

PATEL. My crew are just "batting" down the hatches to keep out the sea. *(Calls to GEOFFREY.)* All right Number One! That will do. *(GEOFFREY stops banging.)*

MRS. W. We haven't hit anything, have we?

PATEL. No, it's just a very bad storm, force ten— *(GEOFFREY throws down lever in despair.)* or even ten and a half.

MRS. W. For such a storm it feels remarkably steady.

PATEL. That is because you are very quick to get your sea legs. Now may I suggest you are sitting down again?

MRS. W. Very well Captain, I have every confidence in you.

PATEL. *(Guides MRS. WAYNEFLETE back to her chair.)* I have to go back to the Bridge work now — it is my turn at the big wheel, you know, one man on, one man off.

MRS. W. Is it your watch?

PATEL. *(Shows it to her.)* Oh yes. Bought it in Delhi — Omega — eleven-thirty. *(He goes into hall, closing the door behind him.)* Can she hear me through this door?

DEIRDRE. I doubt it.

PATEL. *(Sinks to his knees & prays.)* Hari Krishna, Hari Krishna, Our Father in Heaven, Shalom, Allah el Akbar.....

GEOFFREY. *(Stops him in full flow.)* Hang on a minute. What religion are you?

PATEL. At times of great crisis, it is best to keep in with all the important people. *(GEOFFREY sinks to his knees beside PATEL)*

CURTAIN

ACT TWO
Scene One

The same — two weeks later.

> *GEOFFREY is sitting by the radio with headphones on in the recreation room. GRINDLE, DEIRDRE and JOE sit anxiously waiting for GEOFFREY to speak.*

GEOFFREY. *(twiddling knobs of radio)* Damn this thing keeps going dead.

DEIRDRE. Those batteries have been fading for the past two weeks, you said they were guaranteed for two years.

JOE. They were probably six years old when he bought them.

DEIRDRE. More than likely.

GEOFFREY. Taking his side again — Shush. *(GEOFFREY listens intently.)*

JOE. Got something?

GEOFFREY. It keeps coming and going.

DEIRDRE. No word of a missing M.P. yet darling?

GEOFFREY. No.

PATEL. What about a missing milkman?

GEOFFREY. Hardly like to make the World News.

JOE. On the other hand, local M.P. disappears with milkman should help to catch the Speaker's eye.

GEOFFREY. *(Removes headphones.)* It's gone dead again.

GRINDLE. At least we are adjusting to living down here.

JOE. As long as the oxygen lasts.

DEIRDRE. How long will that be?

JOE. Hopefully longer than the batteries.

GEOFFREY. At least three months, as long as we don't get too active and talk our heads off. I mean your mother's frequent readings of the Forsyte Saga to Grindle must have cost us at least two weeks.

DEIRDRE. She reads it very nicely. And it keeps her happy.

GEOFFREY. Oh I am glad about that, it makes it all worthwhile, another fifteen thousand pounds and I could have bolted another shelter on the end of this one — a Granny Shelter for Mummy.

DEIRDRE. Well you wanted to see what the snags were, so now you know — my mother.

GEOFFREY. Well you must admit it, it is a bit trying for us all, trapped down here with her.

DEIRDRE. What harm is she doing?

GEOFFREY. I don't know, I don't even know where she is.

DEIRDRE. Last time I spoke to her she was going to her cabin to dress for dinner.

JOE. What did you say about bolting another shelter on?

GEOFFREY. They're designed to be joined together like railway carriages.

JOE. You mean with communicating doors?

GEOFFREY. Hatchways, yes.

JOE. Has this got one?

GEOFFREY. Behind the kitchen cupboard.

JOE. You mean to say we've been stuck down here all this time with a door you could open?

GEOFFREY. Yes, straight into twenty-five feet of solid earth and rock.

JOE. We could have dug out by now.

GEOFFREY. What with? We haven't got a shovel.

JOE. You got fingers and spoons. They weren't issued with bloody shovels at Colditz. They didn't go up to the Commandant and say, "Excuse me, Fritz, can I have a shovel." They used their ingenuity — tin cans, cups, anything. Come on. *(He runs into kitchen, followed by the others.)* Grab whatever you can. *(Picks up lever en route.)* Deirdre, Grindle, shift that table! *(They do so, JOE strains with the cupboard.)* How do you move this thing?

GEOFFREY. *(pushing him aside)* Here, let me — stand back, stand back. It's electronic. *(Presses button & the cupboard slides back to reveal a large metal door.)*

JOE. Bloody marvellous. Where's Patel?

(Lights dim & go up again.)

GEOFFREY. He's on his way, stand back, stand back. *(Opens metal door.)* There you are.

JOE. *(taking off shirt)* Right.

DEIRDRE. I don't know how you are going to dig through that without the proper tools.

JOE. *(Flexes his muscles.)* Feel that, darling.

GEOFFREY. We'll take your word for it.

JOE. I was an apprentice cable layer for ten years. *(Looks at watch.)* Now then Geoffrey, make a note in that log of yours. At 22.30 hours Joe Parker starts the break out. *(He gets 2 dessert spoons from the drawer & attacks the wall of earth.)*

(PATEL enters from bathroom.)

DEIRDRE. All the earth's going on the floor.

JOE. Well, put the washing-up bowl under it.

PATEL. My God, what is happening?

DEIRDRE. We're trying to dig our way out, Mr. Patel.

JOE. Here, you and Geoffrey have a go with these and I'll have a go with this lever.

PATEL. *(looking at the spoon)* Ugh!

DEIRDRE. What's the matter?

PATEL. This one's got custard on it. *(He goes to the sink to wash it.)*

DEIRDRE. Come on Geoffrey. *(GEOFFREY & JOE dig at the earth.)*

GRINDLE. *(to DEIRDRE)* Joe is very strong, don't you think?

DEIRDRE. Yes. Why don't you go and put little Charles to bed now, Grindle?

GRINDLE. Yes all right, Mrs. Jones. He doesn't want any more of this. *(She puts the bottle on the table & heads for the bedroom.)*

GEOFFREY. Oh blast.

DEIRDRE. What is it?

GEOFFREY. I've bent my spoon.

DEIRDRE. *(taking it)* I'll get you another one. *(She does so.)* How's it going, Joe?

GEOFFREY. You can see how it's going, dear. Damn, I've done it again. *(He shows DEIRDRE a bent spoon.)*

DEIRDRE. *(She gets another two from the drawer.)* We've only got six dessert, after that we're onto the teaspoons.

JOE. If we can keep this up, we could be out of here by Saturday.

DEIRDRE. If we are, Joe, it will be because of you.

GEOFFREY. *(piqued, handing her another bent spoon)* We're both digging, Deirdre.

DEIRDRE. *(to GEOFFREY — & handing him another spoon)* Yes, but he did think of it first.

PATEL. *(to GEOFFREY)* If you're getting tired, sir, I am now ready to take my turn at the tunnel.

GEOFFREY. *(Hands PATEL his spoon.)* Might be a good idea, I'm a bit too strong in the wrist for this. *(Goes to drinks cupboard.)*

DEIRDRE. I expect you need that, darling, you haven't had one for half an hour.

GEOFFREY. It's a very worrying time, Deirdre.

DEIRDRE. Judging by the empties you worry more than the rest of us.

GEOFFREY. Damnit, I have the responsibility for everyone's survival. I mean, if I've made the slightest mistake in the working of this shelter, I'll be the one who has to carry the can.

DEIRDRE. Unless we get out of here, you won't be carrying it far.

GEOFFREY. Up until ten minutes ago, morale was

remarkably high.

JOE. And it still is. Cheers. *(He downs GEOFFREY's drink.)*

GEOFFREY. Cheers!

(GRINDLE comes out of bedroom & crosses to hall.)

GRINDLE. *(calls)* Mrs. Wayneflete is getting very agitated.

GEOFFREY. What's the matter with her now?

GRINDLE. Nobody has come to take her into dinner.

GEOFFREY. Hard cheese.

DEIRDRE. I'm afraid she'll have to wait.

GEOFFREY. Tell her we've been boarded by Chinese Pirates, and unless she wants her throat cut, tell her to stay in her cabin.

GRINDLE. Very well. *(Starts to go.)*

DEIRDRE. You'll tell her nothing of the sort.

(MRS. WAYNEFLETE sweeps into the hall wearing a formal evening gown & a tiara.)

MRS. W. Where is everyone? We're dreadfully late starting dinner.

GRINDLE. They're all through there, Mrs. Wayneflete.

MRS. W. The Captain will never forgive me if I keep him waiting.

DEIRDRE. Don't worry, Mother. He's busy in there.

MRS. W. I must have a word with him.

GEOFFREY. *(seeing Mrs. W.)* Well, hello Dolly!

MRS. W. *(in the kitchen)* What are we doing in the

stoke hold?

DEIRDRE. What do you mean, Mummy?

MRS. W. *(pointing to JOE)* He said he'd be stripped to the waist stoking the boiler.

GEOFFREY. Would you like a sherry, Mother?

MRS. W. I think I'll wait until dinner.

PATEL. *(saluting MRS. W.)* Good evening, Mrs. Wayneflete, may I compliment you on your lovely frock?

MRS. W. Thank you, Captain. I see the furnace has gone out. Are we having trouble?

PATEL. Yes, a big wave came down the funnel.

MRS. W. It's the longest storm I've ever known. Now make sure you get out all that clinker, Parker.

JOE. I'll do my best, Madam.

PATEL. Get out the clinker, Parker.

JOE. *(saluting)* Aye, aye, Sir.

MRS. W. Fine figure of a man, eh Deirdre?

DEIRDRE. Yes, Mother.

MRS. W. I think I will have that drink, Geoffrey.

GEOFFREY. Yes, Mother.

DEIRDRE. As dinner is obviously going to be delayed, why not take your drink through there and read another chapter.

MRS. W. All right. I've just got to the bit where the odious Soames is banging on Fleur's bedroom door and she won't let him in.

JOE. Sounds a bit steamy, that book of yours.

MRS. W. *(excitedly)* Oooh! He's got a tattoo!!

DEIRDRE. All sailors have tattoos, Mother.

GEOFFREY. Mother! Here's your sherry.

MRS. W. Thank you. *(as she goes)* We had a gardner

once who had "The Sinking of the Bismark."

GEOFFREY. Good Lord, where?

MRS. W. In Stoke Poges. *(She goes into recreation room.)*

PATEL. My hand is beginning to ache, would you care to take over my spoon, sir?

GEOFFREY. In a minute. I haven't finished my drink yet.

JOE. *(He suddenly hits a metallic substance with his lever.)* Bloody hell.

DEIRDRE. What is it?

JOE. Dunno — it sounds like metal.

GEOFFREY. *(rushing over)* For God's sake be careful, *(Gingerly feels the substance.)* It is metal.

DEIRDRE. What could it be?

GEOFFREY. Probably from the last war, an unexploded bomb.

JOE. Blimey. *(They all retreat. GEOFFREY closes the door.)* That would've been a bit ironic — trying to dodge the bomb from the next war and getting clobbered by one from the last. *(Goes to pour himself a drink.)*

GEOFFREY. Bit of luck that's in next door's garden. If it had been under here, when they dropped the shelter into place we'd have lost the house.

PATEL. Not to mention the odd life. It could have been mine. I was standing there when they dropped the shelter in.

GEOFFREY. Good job Allah was watching over you.

PATEL. Yes, but I'm afraid it would have been only a cursory glance, I am a Hindu.

GEOFFREY. Oh well, the Big White Chief of the

Hindus then.

DEIRDRE. *(pointed)* Darling, he's not a *red* Indian.

PATEL. No, I am a Conservative Indian.

GEOFFREY. Ah.

JOE. Well that's put the kybosh on things. Let's hope the drink lasts as long as the oxygen.

GEOFFREY. I think Deirdre, that this little development vindicates my reluctance to mention that door, in the first place.

DEIRDRE. We can all be wise after the event, darling.

PATEL. After such a miraculous escape, I would like to pray to Krishna, you do not mind, do you?

GEOFFREY. Good heavens no, every little helps.

PATEL. I will pray for our deliverance. *(He kneels & mumbles a prayer.)*

JOE. Who are you praying to?

PATEL. Krishna. *(then aloud)* Hari Krishna — Hari Krishna.

(There is a loud knocking on the door.)

JOE. He doesn't hang about, does he?

DEIRDRE. Who could it be at this time of the night?

GEOFFREY. Darling, we are 25 feet down underground, under solid rock and earth. It can't possibly be anyone unless it's a hobbit for Grindle.

JOE. What the 'ells an 'hobbit?

PATEL. Perhaps it could be a small animal?

(There are more knocks.)

DEIRDRE. Not so small.

PATEL. Hari Krishna, Hari Krishna.... *(JOE joins the chant.)*

GEOFFREY. Oh this is ridiculous. Joe, see who it is.

JOE. It's your house. You have a look.

DEIRDRE. Well go on dear. *(GEOFFREY picks up lever.)* What's that for?

GEOFFREY. If I don't like the look of it, I'm going to hit it. *(He crosses to the door & opens it gingerly.)* Good Lord.

(RAYMOND BLAKE steps in. He is wearing a silk dressing gown with monogram & has a glass of champagne in his hand.)

RAYMOND. Hello there. *(calling over his shoulder)* Sonia, they're still up.

GEOFFREY. *(blankly)* It's the Blakes.

JOE. From next door?

RAYMOND. Hello old boy.

GEOFFREY. Hello.

RAYMOND. Hello, Mrs. Jones. *(Shakes her hand & looks around.)* Yes, we've got the de luxe model as well.

GEOFFREY. How long have you had your shelter?

RAYMOND. They completed the installation yesterday. So we're just trying it out. I'll go and call Sonia.

GEOFFREY. Don't bother now, it's rather late.

RAYMOND. No trouble. She'd love to see your place. *(He exits.)*

PATEL. So, this is only a semi-detached shelter?

DEIRDRE. Darling, do we have to have them over?

GEOFFREY. Well, it's nearly eleven. I couldn't very well

say we were going out. It'll just be a quick drink and "goodnight."

JOE. You can forget mine, I'm off now.

GEOFFREY. Stay where you are. *(Bars the door.)*

JOE. What's up with you?

GEOFFREY. If we use his exit, he'll know we can't use ours.

DEIRDRE. Well we can't, the handle's broken.

GEOFFREY. I'm not telling him that. Imagine if the papers got hold of that — "Designer trapped in his own shelter." — Make me look like an idiot.

JOE. Only if they print your picture as well.

GEOFFREY. You will all stay where you are.

JOE. Any chance of Patel and me getting a decent house on another estate if we keep quiet?

GEOFFREY. I'll — I'll think about it.

JOE. Thinking isn't quite enough.

RAYMOND. *(off)* Just coming.

GEOFFREY. *(hastily)* All right, you have my word as an M.P.

PATEL. We were safer when he was thinking about it.

(RAYMOND & SONIA enter. She is very glamourous in her housecoat & fluffy slippers. RAYMOND has a glass of champagne.)

SONIA. Good evening all.

GEOFFREY. How nice to see you, Mrs. Blake.

SONIA. "Sonia" please.

RAYMOND. Yes, in view of the situation, I think we

could dispense with the formalities, don't you Deirdre, it is Deirdre isn't it?

DEIRDRE. Er, yes.

RAYMOND. You don't look too sure.

DEIRDRE. Of course I'm sure.

GEOFFREY. This is Joe Parker, our telephone engineer.

JOE. And chief stoker.

GEOFFREY. This is my wife. And that's Clive Patel.

PATEL. Yes, we have met.

SONIA. No wonder we haven't had any milk for a couple of weeks, look Raymond, it's the milkman.

RAYMOND. Very altruistic Geoff, trying to save the multitudes.

GEOFFREY. One does one's best.

GEOFFREY. Would you like a drink, Sonia?

SONIA. Why not?

GEOFFREY. *(going to the bar)* I think we've got everything.

RAYMOND. She's quite keen on the old "Matoose Rosie," aren't you, Sonia?

SONIA. That, or "Tio Peep."

GEOFFREY. I haven't got any Mateuse.

RAYMOND. Run out already?

GEOFFREY. I never took it on board actually, however I can do you a "Tio Peep."

DEIRDRE. *(correcting him)* "Pepe" dear.

GEOFFREY. *(annoyed)* I know, Deirdre.

JOE. I'll have a Martini Bianco, two lumps of ice, a hint of mint and a slice of lemon.

GEOFFREY. Why don't you pi — push off?

JOE. Suits me. Goodnight all. *(to RAYMOND)* Mind if I

use your exit?

RAYMOND. What's wrong with yours?

GEOFFREY. *(hurriedly)* Nothing. *(to JOE)* Surely you can take a joke, old man? *(Puts an arm around his shoulder.)* Was it two lumps of ice?

JOE. Big ones.

GEOFFREY. Help yourself.

(MRS. WAYNEFLETE calls out.)

MRS. W. Would you join me in a hand of bezique, Captain?

PATEL. One moment please! I am just welcoming some new passengers on board!!

MRS. W. Some new faces, what a treat! *(She gets up with her knitting & trails the wool-bag across the hall as she goes.)*

RAYMOND. You been having trouble with your oxygen?

GEOFFREY. No... Why?

RAYMOND. You all sound a bit barmy.

DEIRDRE. My mother thinks she's on a cruise and that the milkman is the Captain and that Joe here is a stoker.

GEOFFREY. And that seems to keep her happy.

RAYMOND. Doesn't take much does it?

MRS. W. *(Enters kitchen.)* How do you do? I'm Mrs. Wayneflete.

RAYMOND. *(shaking her hand)* How do you do, Raymond Blake.

MRS. W. I wasn't aware we'd docked.

DEIRDRE. We haven't.

Mrs. W. Then how did you get aboard?

Geoffrey. Bum boat.

Raymond. Bum boat.

Mrs. W. Where?

Raymond. *(to DEIRDRE)* Where?

Deirdre. Tangiers.

Raymond. *(to MRS. W.)* Tangiers.

Mrs. W. Put down that gang plank, Captain, I'm going into the bazaar to change my jellabi.

Sonia. Your what?

Geoffrey. You can't, Mother!

Mrs. W. Why not?

Geoffrey. The Captain forbids it.

Mrs. W. *(to PATEL)* Why?

Patel. *(to GEOFFREY)* Why?

Geoffrey. There's an outbreak of yellow fever.

Patel. Bright yellow.

Mrs. W. Good heavens. *(to RAYMOND & SONIA)* Is that so?

Raymond. Oh yes, shocking, they're dropping like flies.

Sonia. We were lucky to get out alive.

Mrs. W. Have you been properly innoculated?

Raymond. I should say we have, we could hardly sit in the bumboat!

Mrs. W. *(Notices the strand of wool.)* I seem to be connected to the lounge.

Deirdre. Shall I cut it for you, Mother?

Mrs. W. No, no. I'll knit my way back. *(She wanders back, knitting.)*

Raymond. *(Drains his glass.)* Pardon me if I go and get a

refill of the old bubbly.

GEOFFREY. I've got plenty of champagne.

RAYMOND. Krug '68?

GEOFFREY. No, but a very reasonable Moet.

RAYMOND. We find the cheaper champagne always gives us a headache, don't we, Sonia?

SONIA. Gives me a funny tummy.

RAYMOND. Hasn't done a lot for your face. Be back in a jiff, Geoff. *(Exits through hatch door.)*

(GRINDLE enters living room & goes to hall.)

GRINDLE. *(calling)* Mrs. Jones?

DEIRDRE. Yes, what is it, Grindle?

GRINDLE. I think little Charles would like the rest of his bottle.

DEIRDRE. Well go and put the heater on and I'll do this feed.

MRS. W. *(as DEIRDRE passes her)* Have they repaired the boiler yet?

DEIRDRE. Not yet, Mother. *(She disappears into the bedroom with GRINDLE.)*

GEOFFREY. *(to SONIA)* A little top up?

SONIA. I never say no.

JOE. Ever been to Benidorm?

SONIA. Yes, I did some beach shots a couple of years ago for one of Raymond's magazines.

JOE. Which one?

SONIA. "Playpen."

JOE. *(impressed)* "Playpen" — are you in that?

SONIA. From time to time.

JOE. I've bought that a few times but I don't remember seeing you.

SONIA. Well I sometimes wear a wig.

JOE. Oh well that could explain it.

GEOFFREY. You weren't wearing a wig on the Matterhorn, just ski boots and a pom-pom hat.

DEIRDRE. When did you see that?

GEOFFREY. Jerry Hanssen brought it into the office. He likes that sort of thing.

DEIRDRE. So it seems.

SONIA. I was Miss January in that one.

PATEL. No, February actually.

SONIA. Oh you bought it as well, did you?

PATEL. Yes — I pinned it on the wall of the depot. Everybody was very jealous of the fact that I was your milkman.

SONIA. Oh, isn't that nice, 'ere when you didn't turn up I got quite worried. I thought something had happened to you.

PATEL. It did. I have been incarcerated down here for two weeks, in fact I am surprised you didn't enquire as to my whereabouts.

SONIA. Well, Raymond and I did have a long discussion about what might have happened.

PATEL. Already I am feeling better.

SONIA. And then Raymond decided you might have scarpered with the takings.

PATEL. It worries me the reputation the Express Dairy is having, they are excellent employers.

JOE. Well, when this little exercise is over I shall be straight down to the news-agents for your backnumbers.

SONIA. Oooh. Pity you weren't around when we needed some beef-cake. *(Playfully pokes him in the stomach.)* Oh, have you been pumping iron?

JOE. *(embarrassed)* Just the tires on the motor bike.

SONIA. You ever thought about doing some male modeling?

JOE. Bit poncy that, isn't it?

SONIA. No it's not, you should.

PATEL. Could I have a glass of milk please?

GEOFFREY. You and your damned milk — you'll have to have the powdered stuff.

SONIA. You short of milk?

GEOFFREY. Yes, 'fraid we are.

SONIA. You really are doing it thoroughly — hardship and all. If you want milk go next door and help yourself.

PATEL. I am most grateful.

SONIA. Tell Raymond to give you a bottle.

PATEL. I will, thank you. *(Exits through hatch door.)*

GEOFFREY. That's very good of you, Mrs. Blake.

SONIA. Sonia — please!

GEOFFREY. Sonia, you know Sonia, you've been living next door for a couple of years and we've never actually been in your place.

SONIA. We've never been in yours, either.

GEOFFREY. True.

SONIA. I did wave to your wife once. She was leaning out the window when they delivered our gas boiler.

GEOFFREY. Yes, she mentioned that.

SONIA. Funny you know Geoffrey, since we moved in, this is the first really deep chat we've had.

GEOFFREY. Foolish isn't it, to be so reserved.

SONIA. Raymond always said you was a toffee-nose but I don't think you are.

GEOFFREY. People are rather like a row of houses. *(He puts a foot on the chair & leans forward.)* You never know who lives in them until you knock on the door.

JOE. If you lean over much further you'll be climbing in her window.

GEOFFREY. I'd quite like to see your place, perhaps I could go up through your shelter and have a look.

JOE. Good thinking, Geoffrey, can I come too?

SONIA. I'll give you a guided tour.

(RAYMOND re-enters with an open bottle of champagne.)

RAYMOND. Sorry I've been so long, but I've just caught a newsflash. Some idiot on our side has fired a test missile and it's gone out of control.

GEOFFREY. I've been campaigning in House for stricter controls on tests: this sort of thing was always on the cards, where is it?

RAYMOND. Floating around 300 miles up with a wonky computer supplied by the firm who put in the lowest quote.

JOE. Blimy, it could fall on England.

RAYMOND. No, it could fall on Russia, it passes over Siberia about every half an hour.

GEOFFREY. No need to panic, I shouldn't really tell you this but a friend of mine on the Defence Committee *(Then taps the side of his nose confidentially.....)*

RAYMOND. Jewish?

GEOFFREY. No, I mean keep it under your hat: he tells me this sort of thing has happened before and they always burn themselves out on land, or in the sea.

RAYMOND. Well if anything does go wrong, I've got all my money tied up in gold bars in Switzerland. *(He shows them a key which hangs from a gold chain around his neck.)* My safety deposit box — the key to the future.

SONIA. It's a real gold key too.

GEOFFREY. Very impressive, but some of us do pay our taxes.

SONIA. Funny you know, both our shelters are the same, but ours feels totally different.

RAYMOND. I think it's our flying ducks over the mantlepiece.

GEOFFREY. Flying ducks?

RAYMOND. Yes. It gives it that *je ne sais quoi.*

SONIA. Would you like to see them?

GEOFFREY. Oh, I don't know.

RAYMOND. Go on Sonia, take him round.

SONIA. Come on Geoffrey.

GEOFFREY. All right, but I think all the others would like to see them too.

JOE. Yes they would.

SONIA. They can see them later.

RAYMOND. *(as SONIA & GEOFFREY go towards the hatch)* Don't forget to show him the sauna and jacuzzi.

GEOFFREY. Sauna and jacuzzi? *(He eagerly follows SONIA off.)*

JOE. Must feel odd being married to a sex symbol.

RAYMOND. She's got used to it.

JOE. *(laughing)* Yes — but don't you ever get jealous?

RAYMOND. Why?

JOE. Well think of all those men ogling your wife.

RAYMOND. I cry all the way to the bank.

(GRINDLE enters from bedroom with empty baby bottle, she heads for the kitchen but is stopped by RAYMOND in the hall.)

RAYMOND. 'ello, 'ello, I don't think I've had the pleasure, have I?

GRINDLE. Oh hello Mr. Blake.

RAYMOND. Oh, you know me?

GRINDLE. I've seen you driving down the road in that big Yankee car.

RAYMOND. Snap. I've seen you walking the pram, it's one of the prettiest sights in Northolt. How about a drop of this Krug champagne?

GRINDLE. Yes, thank you.

RAYMOND. *(to JOE)* Glass for the lady. *(JOE gets glass. To GRINDLE.)* You know with a figure like yours, you are wasted here.

GRINDLE. This is what I am trained for.

RAYMOND. What I have in mind you wouldn't have to train for.

GRINDLE. What is that?

RAYMOND. I'm in publishing. I've got a magazine called "Playpen."

GRINDLE. Oh, for the babies?

RAYMOND. No, no. It's a man's magazine.

GRINDLE. No, I don't read that sort of thing.

RAYMOND. I'm not talking about you reading it. How

about you being in it?

GRINDLE. I don't think I have the figure.

RAYMOND. You're joking. You could make a fortune.

GRINDLE. What would I have to do?

RAYMOND. Practically nothing, it's a piece of cake. You don't know how lucky you are. With your figure, you could be Miss June, busting out all over.

JOE. I suppose it doesn't occur to you that she might be the sort of girl that doesn't want to take her clothes off.

RAYMOND. If she was 'centre-fold' she'd get a thousand pounds.

GRINDLE. *(impressed)* A thousand pounds?

RAYMOND. And if the legs are half as good as I think they are, even more. *(GRINDLE raises her skirt to show her thighs.)* Fifteen hundred.

JOE. She's got a perfectly good job already.

GRINDLE. But very little money. *(RAYMOND & GRINDLE drink.)*

(DEIRDRE enters from the bedroom — heads for the kitchen but stops when she sees them in the hall.)

DEIRDRE. Oh, am I interrupting something? *(GRINDLE grabs the baby's bottle.)*

JOE. I'm afraid you're too late, you've just lost your nanny to the world of "playpen."

DEIRDRE. *(shocked)* Grindle, is this true?

GRINDLE. *(with a slight laugh)* I think he was only joking.

RAYMOND. I've never been so serious in my life.

DEIRDRE. *(stiffly)* I think I should point out that I will require three months notice. *(She goes into kitchen.)*

(SONIA & GEOFFREY enter laughing together & carrying garish glasses. GEOFFREY is the worse for drink.)

GEOFFREY. Oh hello, we've just been next door.
DEIRDRE. *(coldly)* Been what next door?
GEOFFREY. Looking over their shelter.
DEIRDRE. Fascinating.
GEOFFREY. It's quite different actually.
DEIRDRE. I'm sure it is.
GEOFFREY. They've even got a chandelier.
SONIA. It sort of goes with the velvet drapes.
GEOFFREY. Oh absolutely, and I had a quick look at her jacuzzi.
DEIRDRE. Hasn't everyone?
RAYMOND. What did you think of the water bed?
DEIRDRE. Water bed?
GEOFFREY. Yes. If I was on my honeymoon, I'd be seasick
SONIA. You would if you were with me. *(They laugh. DEIRDRE stares stonily.)*
GEOFFREY. *(to SONIA)* Er, would you like to see the baby?
SONIA. Yes, I love babies, especially little ones.
GEOFFREY. Come along then.
DEIRDRE. I'd rather you didn't, dear—
SONIA. Raymond and I have been dying to have a baby, haven't we Raymond?
RAYMOND. Yes. We haven't managed it yet.

Sonia. It's not for want of trying.

Geoffrey. Come along, Sonia.

Deirdre. I've only just got him off to sleep.

Sonia. We'll be as quiet as mice. *(GEOFFREY leads her into bedroom.)*

Raymond. Deirdre, perhaps you'd care to see how the other half lives?

Deirdre. I've got a pretty good idea, thank you Mr. Blake.

Raymond. How about you, Grindle?

Grindle. Oh yes.

Deirdre. She's on duty.

Grindle. Wednesday's supposed to be my evening off.

Deirdre. *(tetchily)* Oh all right, go.

Grindle. Thank you.

Raymond. After you, my dear. *(They both exit.)*

Joe. Like a drink?

Deirdre. Very much.

Joe. What'll it be?

Deirdre. Anything, and make it a large one.

Joe. You're a bit fed up aren't you?

Deirdre. Is it that obvious?

Joe. It's been obvious for days.

Deirdre. It's not very pleasant to see your husband making a fool of himself.

Joe. I'd say he was making a fool of you, and you don't deserve it.

Deirdre. Thanks Joe.

Joe. If you've got no objection, I'm about to make a fool of myself.

DEIRDRE. How?

JOE. I'm going to put my arm around you and kiss you
— very hard.

DEIRDRE. Joe — don't.

JOE. *(taking hold of her)* And when you want me to stop
just kick me on the shins. *(He kisses her. She raises her foot &
then entwines it round her other leg.)*

*(During this passionate kiss MRS. WAYNEFLETE enters
from kitchen.)*

MRS. W. *(mildly surprised)* Deirdre, really. *(JOE &
DEIRDRE break.)*

DEIRDRE. Couldn't you knock, Mother? *(They kiss
again.)*

MRS. W. Deirdre! I too have had the occasional ship-
board romance, but in my day we were more discreet
about it.

JOE. I'm sorry, Mrs. Wayneflete, it was all my fault.

DEIRDRE. It wasn't his fault at all, Mother, now can we
just forget it?

MRS. W. I'm not blaming you, dear. He's a very attractive stoker, and who knows, if I was forty years
younger....

DEIRDRE. Mother!

MRS. W. You didn't invent it you know. Where's
Geoffrey?

JOE. He's gone off with the Entertainments Officer.

MRS. W. I'm still waiting for my after-dinner coffee.

DEIRDRE. We haven't had dinner yet.

MRS. W. Haven't we? May I suggest you put your shirt

on again young man, it's stirring old memories. As I said, if I were twenty years younger....

DEIRDRE. Mother please!!

JOE. *(backing out)* Excuse me.

MRS. W. You don't have to leave on my account.

JOE. I'm just going to shed a tear for Nelson. *(He exits to hall & heads for bathroom.)*

MRS. W. Is that the same as pointing Percy to the porcelain?

DEIRDRE. *(closing the hatch door)* I'll make us some coffee.

MRS. W. I take it Geoffrey knows nothing of er —

DEIRDRE. No, he doesn't.

MRS. W. Well don't worry, I won't breath a word.

DEIRDRE. I don't think it matters one way or the other actually.

MRS. W. Oh well, if you remember, I did warn you at the time, you could have done better for yourself.

DEIRDRE. Well, it's too late now, isn't it? *(She starts to cry.)*

MRS. W. *(Goes to comfort her.)* There, there dear. I think this cruise is getting you down. Mark you, the weather's been so disappointing I shan't be sorry to get back to England. *(DEIRDRE is still crying.)* Just think of all the lovely things we've got to look forward to; The Flower Show—

DEIRDRE. *(interrupting)* Oh Mother, stop it. You just don't understand.

MRS. W. I understand more than you think. *(She gives DEIRDRE a handkerchief.)* Blow your nose. *(DEIRDRE does so as...)*

*(RAYMOND & GRINDLE enter through the hatch door. GRIN-
   DLE closes the door behind them.)*

RAYMOND. Here we are again. *(They all lift their glasses.)*

*(There is a deafening explosion. The hatch door to the Blakes'
   shelter flies open & a cloud of dust blows through. MRS. W.
   picks up the bottle and looks at the label to see what has given
   her such a kick. PATEL enters through the door, dazed
   & dishevelled.)*

PATEL. It is the end.
RAYMOND. For Christ's sake, shut the door. *(He throws
himself at the door & clamps it shut.*
MRS. W. *(to PATEL)* Captain, what have you hit?
PATEL. Nothing for you to worry about, Mrs. Wayne-
flete, we have just hit the end of the jetty.

*(The lights dim & go up. GEOFFREY & SONIA run out of the
   bedroom to the kitchen.)*

GEOFFREY. *(shouts)* Hold on, don't panic, I'm coming.

(JOE appears from the bathroom.)

JOE. What was that?
GEOFFREY. *(to DEIRDRE)* Are you all right, darling?
DEIRDRE. Yes Geoffrey.
GEOFFREY. Thank God.
RAYMOND. You know what's happened? That rocket's
fallen on Russia.

PATEL. Rocket?

DEIRDRE. What rocket?

GEOFFREY. Apparently one of our missiles went out of control.

DEIRDRE. How do you know?

RAYMOND. I heard it on the radio.

PATEL. If it landed in Russia why did it go "bang" here?

RAYMOND. Because they've sent one back in retaliation.

SONIA. At least we're all in one piece and that's all that matters.

RAYMOND. We wouldn't have been if we'd been in our shelter. The hatch in the garden was still open.

PATEL. And to think I was in there! Hari Krishna! Hari Krishna!

RAYMOND. Pull yourself together, Patel. Have you lost your bottle?

PATEL. *(producing a bottle)* No, I have it here. I am lucky to be alive. The stairway is blocked by bricks and rubble.

RAYMOND. Come on Geoff, we'll use your exit. *(Heads for the stairs.)* I've got to phone Switzerland.

JOE. You'll be lucky.

GEOFFREY. You can't get out that way, the hatch won't open.

RAYMOND. Why not?

GEOFFREY. The handle's fallen off!

RAYMOND. I don't believe it.

JOE. We'll tunnel up through yours.

GEOFFREY. Are you mad? If that was an atomic warhead it'll be radioactive.

RAYMOND. Well if it is radioactive, then Patel's radioactive. Look, he's covered in it from head to foot.

PATEL. *(Starts brushing the dust off.)* No, no, this is just plaster from the flying ducks. *(Picks a bit off.)* Look, this is a bit of beak.

GEOFFREY. Don't bring it near me.

RAYMOND. Too late to worry now, this place is full of dust. *(He wipes some off the table.)* See? *(Everyone starts talking at once except MRS. WAYNEFLETE, who bangs the table with the champagne bottle.)*

MRS. W. Silence! There must be no panic. Remember we're British.

PATEL. Yes, of course.

GEOFFREY. *(shutting hatch door)* Why did you have to leave your bloody hatch open?

RAYMOND. Well it's better than having a hatch that doesn't open at all.

GEOFFREY. Don't you speak to me like that in front of my wife.

MRS. W. Geoffrey, calm down. There is nothing to worry about.

GEOFFREY. Nothing to worry about? Civilization as we know it has just come to an end.

MRS. W. The Captain has already indicated that there is no cause for alarm.

GEOFFREY. *(blowing his top)* He's not the flaming Captain, he's the bloody milkman.

MRS. W. *(to DEIRDRE)* I'm afraid he's gone to pieces, dear.

GEOFFREY. You stupid woman! We've spent the best

years of our lives looking after you, shielding you from reality — from the truth — but this is the end of the line. So if you can possibly open the door to that mothball mind of yours for just one second I might be able to appraise you of our desperate and tragic situation.

DEIRDRE. Geoffrey, I forbid you.

GEOFFREY. *(ignoring her)* We are not on a cruise, we have never been on a cruise. We are in fact in an atomic shelter, 25 feet below ground. And the Third World War has just started. At this very moment radioactive dust is settling over London like a shroud over a dead body and to make matters worse there is no way out, we're here — entombed for eternity. Now do you understand?

MRS. W. Yes dear. *(rising)* Captain, would you care for a hand of cards in the lounge? *(GEOFFREY collapses.)*

CURTAIN

ACT TWO
Scene Two

The same, one week later.

> *There is an evening meal in progress. DEIRDRE, GEOF-*
> *FREY, RAYMOND & SONIA are at the kitchen table.*
> *JOE & GRINDLE are eating in the hall. MRS. W. and*
> *PATEL are playing cards in the recreation room.*

GEOFFREY. *(picking at his food)* Deirdre, do we have to
have sultana pudding again?

DEIRDRE. I thought it was your favourite.

GEOFFREY. *(angrily)* Not after a week of it.

DEIRDRE. Well, there's only one other pudding left.

GEOFFREY. What's that?

DEIRDRE. Blancmange.

GEOFFREY. Ugh.

SONIA. Oh come on. try a spoonful, you've got to keep
your strength up.

GEOFFREY. For what?

RAYMOND. *(reaching out)* I'll have it then.

GEOFFREY. *(grabbing the plate)* No you won't! It's
mine!!

RAYMOND. You just said you didn't want it.

GEOFFREY. I don't, but it's mine and I can do what I
like with it.

81

DEIRDRE. Geoffrey, please.

GEOFFREY.   GEOFFREY. *(ignoring her)* We agreed to ration ourselves — what's yours is yours and what's mine is mine, and I'll dispose of it when and where I like.

DEIRDRE. Perhaps he'll have it later.

GEOFFREY. I won't have it at all!! *(He flings it with a crash into the sink.)* There, have I made my point?

RAYMOND. Very clearly. No wonder the Speaker doesn't want to catch your eye. You're a bloody lunatic.

GEOFFREY. If you remember, we didn't cater for you two down here.

RAYMOND. *(pointing to the sink)* You call that catering?

GEOFFREY. If you've any complaints, you can always leave, there's the door.

RAYMOND. You'd like to see the back of us, wouldn't you?

GEOFFREY. If there's a choice, it's preferable to the front.

SONIA. *(piqued)* No one's ever said that to me before.

GEOFFREY. *(hurriedly)* I'm sorry, Sonia, of course I didn't mean it. It's just the damned strain of it all.

RAYMOND. It's a strain for us too. We're all in the same boat.

GEOFFREY. And it happens to be mine.

(The baby cries.)

GEOFFREY. Oh God, I need a drink.

SONIA. Me too, please.

DEIRDRE. Now you've upset Charles.

GEOFFREY. Grindle, it's time the baby was in bed.

GRINDLE. Yes, all right, I'm just finishing my pudding.

GEOFFREY. I want you to do it now!

GRINDLE. Very well. *(She comes into the kitchen & picks up the carry cot.)*

MRS. W. There, I'm out Captain.

PATEL. The cards were running your way, Mrs. Wayneflete.

MRS. W. My deal, I think.

RAYMOND. *(Puts an arm around GRINDLE's waist as she picks up carry cot.)* Goodnight little man. *(He bursts into song.)*

SWEETEST LITTLE FELLER, EVERYBODY KNOWS
DON'T KNOW WHAT TO CALL HIM
'COS HE MIGHT BE ONE OF THOSE......!

GEOFFREY. How dare you! *(pushing him aside)*

RAYMOND. Here — watch it!

GEOFFREY. If you don't mind, I would like to say good night to my son.

RAYMOND. Help yourself.

GEOFFREY. Sleep well, little man. *(The baby cries.)* Shut up. *(RAYMOND laughs.)* And you.

DEIRDRE. Grindle, I'll be through in a minute.

GRINDLE. Yes, OK Deirdre. *(She exits to nursery.)*

GEOFFREY. "OK Deirdre?" Damned cheek.

JOE. What's eating you?

GEOFFREY. We don't pay the staff to be familiar.

JOE. I see, keeping up the class war to the end, Geoffrey?

SONIA. Frankly, I'm in favour of a bit of class.

GEOFFREY. Thank you, Sonia.

DEIRDRE. There's no such thing as class, Sonia, it's an illusion brought on purely by the manner in which one speaks. If I've learned anything in the past three weeks I've learned that.

JOE. Pity one finds it out too late. *(stops)* Here, hark at me — "Pity *one* finds out...." I'm picking it up now.

DEIRDRE. *(tongue in cheek)* That's a turn up, innit Joe?

JOE. I could've gone out happier three weeks ago.

DEIRDRE. Why?

JOE. 'Cos I didn't know what I was missing.

GEOFFREY. Well, why should you miss it? I notice there has been a lot of talk but very little action.

DEIRDRE. You should understand that, dear.

GEOFFREY. Well darling, if you fancy the artisan type?

JOE. Big words, Geoffrey. *(to DEIRDRE)* I think he means a bit of "rough" dear.

GEOFFREY. Come on then, do you or don't you?

DEIRDRE. Do you really want to know?

GEOFFREY. Yes I do.

DEIRDRE. Very well. *(She grabs JOE & gives him a passionate kiss.)* Does that answer your question?

GEOFFREY. *(piqued)* It most certainly does. *(He puts his glass on the tea-chest, then grabs SONIA & kisses her.)*

RAYMOND. *(suddenly incensed)* Here! That's my wife. Where's your bleeding manners?

SONIA. A lot you care.

RAYMOND. Course I bloody care.

SONIA. That's a laugh. You've had the "hots" for that Scandinavian skivvy ever since we came down here.

GEOFFREY. Hardly the way for a guest to behave in someone else's shelter.

RAYMOND. I'm not here by choice. I'm 'ere because I was bombed out.

GEOFFREY. The point is that you are 'ere and at this moment you owe your life to me.

RAYMOND. You call this life, seeing you sling your spotted dick everywhere — a baby screaming its head off, and that old cuckoo clock in there playing cards with the milkman? I'd rather be dead and buried.

SONIA. We're halfway there now.

JOE. All this bickering only uses up oxygen.

DEIRDRE. Joe's quite right.

GEOFFREY. Joe's always bloody right.

RAYMOND. The oxygen is going to run out sooner or later.

GEOFFREY. And sooner because of you.

RAYMOND. I don't use up any more than you.

GEOFFREY. *(Points at SONIA.)* What about Sonia? Look at the size of those lungs. When we came down here we had enough for three months — due to unforeseen circumstances, for which you're largely responsible, we're not going to make it.

JOE. How do you know?

GEOFFREY. Because we were advised by the Government that it would take months for the dust to blow away.

JOE. How do you know there hasn't been a gale? A couple of good storms might have cleared the whole thing away by now.

RAYMOND. He could be right. Pity you haven't got a

periscope, Geoff. I'd love to have a look.

GEOFFREY. There's nothing to see.

JOE. There might be Red Cross Ambulances, decontamination centres.....

RAYMOND. And anything's better than talking ourselves to death.

GEOFFREY. What do you suggest?

RAYMOND. Someone should claw their way through our rubble, and stick their nose out, then come back and report.

GEOFFREY. Right, good luck. *(Shakes his hand.)* And don't be too long.

RAYMOND. Hang on Geoff. Let's talk it through.

GEOFFREY. What is there to discuss?

RAYMOND. I don't want to hog all the glory if someone wants to volunteer.

JOE. All right, I'll go.

DEIRDRE. No!

GEOFFREY. Deirdre, don't interfere.

DEIRDRE. Joe's a young man, he's got his whole life before him.

GEOFFREY. Right now, he's got no more than the rest of us.

RAYMOND. Your wife's got a point, Geoff. I think it should be the oldest — the one with the least number of years to go. By the way, I'm thirty-eight.

SONIA. *(amazed)* Thirty-eight?

RAYMOND. That's what I just said, you stupid parrot. How about you, Joe?

JOE. Thirty-one.

DEIRDRE. Oh dear, Geoffrey, you're fifty-one.

GEOFFREY. We haven't asked everybody yet. *(Points.)* There's the other room.

DEIRDRE. *(astounded)* You can't expect my mother to shift a ton of rubble and........

GEOFFREY. Don't be a fool, I mean Patel. *(He strides into the hall.)* Captain, can I have a word with you?

PATEL. *(Gets up.)* Mrs. Wayneflete, may I be excused?

MRS. W. Of course, Captain. It's through there and be careful with that flush. *(PATEL joins others in the hall.)*

GEOFFREY. I'll be brief, Patel. We just want to ask you a question.

PATEL. Yes?

GEOFFREY. Tell me, how old are you?

PATEL. Why?

GEOFFREY. Well, it doesn't really matter why.

JOE. 'Course it does. The oldest one of us has been elected to go through that rubble and up through the hatch to see if the air is clear or not.

PATEL. Well good luck Mr. Jones. *(Makes to go.)*

GEOFFREY. No, no Patel. That's you.

PATEL. Suppose I don't come back?

GEOFFREY. Then we'll know. Good luck, Patel. *(PATEL walks slowly towards the hatch in the kitchen.)*

JOE. Chin up, Clive.

DEIRDRE. Best of British.

RAYMOND. All the best, old man.

SONIA. Yeah, all the best.

PATEL. *(Stops in his tracks & turns.)* I should be feeling very honoured. But to my surprise I am not getting that feeling.

GEOFFREY. *(pointing to PATEL's cap)* Patel!

PATEL. Oh yes. *(Puts cap on.)* Express Dairy Company.

DEIRDRE. Darling, you can't send poor Mr. Patel. He's already been blown up once.

PATEL. Heavens yes, I'd forgotten. *(He runs back to recreation room.)*

MRS. W. That was quick, Captain.

PATEL. I didn't want to go.

SONIA. The only fair thing is to draw lots.

RAYMOND. You have to open your big mouth.

JOE. That's a good idea. I reckon that's fair.

GEOFFREY. All right, we'll cut the cards for it. *(He goes to MRS. W.)* Will you give me that pack, Mother?

MRS. W. Are you joining us?

GEOFFREY. In a minute.

RAYMOND. Hang on there, Geoff. I don't want the one off the bottom.

GEOFFREY. *(holding pack out)* I suppose you want to cut them.

JOE. Give them to Mrs. Wayneflete. *(He takes the pack from GEOFFREY & gives it to MRS. WAYNEFLETE.)* Deal us all a card, will you?

MRS. W. What are we playing?

GEOFFREY. Never mind. Just deal. Highest one goes out, right?

RAYMOND. Right. *(MRS. WAYNEFLETE deals four cards on the table — face down. They are about to pick them up.)*

PATEL. Wait! Are aces high, or low?

GEOFFREY. High, right?

RAYMOND. Right. *(He picks up his card & looks at it.)* 3 of clubs.

JOE. *(looking at his card)* 9 of diamonds.

PATEL. *(weakly)* Queen of hearts.

GEOFFREY. Bad luck. *(Picks up his card, looks at it & flings it onto the table.)* Who said aces high?

RAYMOND. You did.

GEOFFREY. Well, that's it.

MRS. W. It's the shortest game of cards I've ever known.

PATEL. *(Steps back.)* Well good luck, Mr. Jones.

JOE. Chin up, Geoffrey.

RAYMOND. All the best.

DEIRDRE. Do be careful, darling.

SONIA. I think you're ever so brave. *(GEOFFREY goes to the sink, puts on bathing cap & rubber gloves.)*

DEIRDRE. *(Gets his golf hat from his golf bag.)* Don't forget this darling.

GEOFFREY. Well darling, this is it. If I don't come back, try and manage without me and bring up little Charles as we both would want. *(Puts on gas mask, then embraces DEIRDRE.)* Goodbye Deirdre.

DEIRDRE. Goodbye Geoffrey. *(GEOFFREY walks to hatch.)*

(There is a loud knocking.)

SONIA. What's that?

JOE. Shush.

MRS. W. What have we hit this time, Captain?

PATEL. Perhaps it is the hobbit for Miss Grindle.

(More knocking on the door. GEOFFREY removes his gas mask.)

JOE. They're using a crowbar, it won't hold out much longer.

GEOFFREY. There's only one thing for it.

DEIRDRE. Geoffrey, you can't hide now.

GEOFFREY. I'm not hiding, I'm getting my golf clubs.

RAYMOND. Golf clubs? The Russians don't play golf.

GEOFFREY. We're not going to play. These are weapons. We're going to hook and slice our way out of trouble.

RAYMOND. On the other hand we could surrender.

GEOFFREY. Never. I'm taking a No. 7 Iron. How about you, Raymond?

RAYMOND. It's a toss up between the Driver and the Sand Iron. How about you, Joe?

JOE. I don't play. I'll stick to this.

GEOFFREY. Don't forget to duck, girls, when we start swinging these things.

DEIRDRE. What good will that do?

JOE. We're going to take a few of them with us.

GEOFFREY. Have you any idea what the Mongolian hoardes do when they over-run a country?

DEIRDRE. I can guess.

SONIA. What do they do?

GEOFFREY. They rape and pillage.

SONIA. Rape and pillage. Oooh. *(She puts lipstick on.)* Hang on, what's pillage?

(Further bangs are heard.)

JOE. It's going, look out. *(They raise their weapons.)*

(The door opens & P.C. BOBBY SMITH enters.)

P.C. Evening all. *(Sees the clubs.)* You're not using those as offensive weapons are you?

GEOFFREY. Er — no.

P.C. Just lay them down. *(They do so.)* Now would there be a Mr. and Mrs. Blake down here?

RAYMOND. Yes, yes, we are.

P.C. I've got a bit of bad news for you, sir.

RAYMOND. Just for me, why not her?

GEOFFREY. Yes, why single him out in the middle of a war?

P.C. What war?

GEOFFREY. The rocket that fell on Russia.

P.C. Don't you follow the news?

DEIRDRE. No, our batteries went flat.

P.C. It fizzled out harmlessly in the Pacific.

DEIRDRE. *(to GEOFFREY)* If you hadn't bought dud batteries we'd have known all this.

P.C. Then you won't have heard about the other major event.

GEOFFREY. No, tell us.

P.C. Norway won the Eurovision Song Contest.

SONIA. They never?

RAYMOND. How does that affect me?

P.C. Sorry sir, it would appear that you, or Mrs. Blake — when you vacated your house — left a pilot light on your gas central heating.

RAYMOND. So?

P.C. Well due to a leak, the whole house filled up with gas and on the evening of the 19th at approximately

10:30 p.m. it blew up.

RAYMOND. *(aghast)* Cobblers?

P.C. No sir, I'm afraid it is perfectly true.

RAYMOND. God.

DEIRDRE. *(Puts her arms around SONIA.)* I'm so sorry.

GEOFFREY. *(to RAYMOND)* It must be a terrible shock, but you're welcome to our spare room, old chap.

RAYMOND. Thanks Geoff. *(They shake hands.)*

GEOFFREY. Not at all, what are neighbours for?

RAYMOND. Come on, Sonia.

SONIA. Neighbours? We got nothing to be neighbours in. *(They exit through hatchway.)*

P.C. *(calling after them)* It's a bit rough out there, why don't you go out through this one? *(Indicates GEOF-FREY's exit.)*

GEOFFREY. I'm afraid it's out of action — our handle fell off.

P.C. Really? *(Walks into hall.)*

JOE. I'll go and tell Grindle the good news. *(Goes through living room, stops by MRS. WAYNEFLETE & PATEL, who are playing cards.)* War's over. We're out.

MRS. W. So am I. Almost. *(JOE exits.)*

PATEL. *(Goes to P.C. in hall.)* Excuse me, are you by any chance looking for a milkman?

P.C. *(examining wall near broken handle)* No thanks, we get ours at the Co-op.

PATEL. That's all right then. *(He goes into living room.)* Mrs. Wayneflete, it's time to be going.

MRS. W. One moment please, another four cards. *(By now, GEOFFREY & DEIRDRE have joined the P.C. in the hall.)*

GEOFFREY. *(Taps oxygen gauge.)* Damn close thing, only enough oxygen for another thirty days.

P.C. We've got one of these shelters installed in the station, sir.

GEOFFREY. Well, let's hope you have better luck with your handle.

P.C. Actually sir, there's a fail safe button just round here that blows the catches off. *(Goes to button.)* Here we are. *(Presses button.)*

(Loud bang & daylight streams in.)

DEIRDRE. You never read instructions.

GEOFFREY. I did.

DEIRDRE. What's the use if you don't understand them? *(calls)* Come along, Mother.

MRS. W. What is it?

PATEL. We are going home, Madam.

MRS. W. *(getting up)* I know, you hit the jetty again.

P.C. Evening, Madam.

MRS. W. Ah Customs. I've nothing to declare. *(She shows him her open handbag.)*

P.C. Pardon, Madam? *(He looks puzzled.)*

MRS. W. *(Starts looking for something.)* Now where did I put the Forsyte Saga?

PATEL. Let me help you. *(Starts looking.)*

DEIRDRE. My mother's been under some strain. I'm afraid she lives in another world.

GEOFFREY. Not a bad one either.

PATEL. Shall I start the milk as from tomorrow?

DEIRDRE. Yes please. I think I'd better have a dozen

large eggs and half a pound of butter.

PATEL. Very good.

P.C. *(to PATEL)* Oh, so it's your milk float there is it?

PATEL. Yes officer.

P.C. Well, it's been causing an obstruction. *(Takes out police pad & writes.)* Name?

PATEL. C. Patel.

P.C. Address?

PATEL. Care of the Express Dairy Company. *(P.C. writes as PATEL speaks.)* You see, I could not drive it away, as I have been incarcerated.

P.C. Whatever they've done to you in India won't wash with me. *(Tears off docket from pad & hands it to PATEL)* You are required to produce this with your Electric Vehicle Driving License at the station within 24 hours.

PATEL. Thank you sir. *(P.C. exits up stairs.)*

(JOE & GRINDLE enter with carry cot. JOE is carrying it, GRINDLE follows.)

GRINDLE. I'll take him now, Joe.

JOE. Oh O.K. *(He hands GRINDLE the carry cot as they reach the bottom of the stairs.)*

DEIRDRE. Give Charles to me. We'll carry him up.

GRINDLE. Oh all right, Mrs. Jones. *(She hands the baby over & walks upstairs.)*

PATEL. *(to MRS. W.)* I can't find your book for looking.

MRS. W. I expect that girl was reading it in the baby's room.

PATEL. I will get it for you. *(Both exit into bedroom.)*

JOE. Well goodbye Mrs. Jones.

DEIRDRE. Oh, goodbye Joe. *(She puts the cot down & shakes JOE's hand.)* We probably won't meet again.

JOE. Don't you want me to reconnect the extension?

GEOFFREY. I don't think there's any hurry for it now.

JOE. Well I suppose this is goodbye.

DEIRDRE. I'll miss you, Joe.

JOE. I'll miss you too, Mrs. Jones.

GEOFFREY. Why don't you go off to Benidorm and "cherchez la femme"?

JOE. I've had a better idea.

GEOFFREY. What, the Bahamas?

JOE. No. I'm taking Grindle to the pictures. *(He runs up the stairs.)*

GEOFFREY. Well old girl, should it ever come to the real thing, we'll know how to deal with it next time.

DEIRDRE. I certainly will. It's straight down to the local for a pint. *(She starts to walk upstairs.)*

GEOFFREY. You don't mean that.

DEIRDRE. Try me darling. *(She exits.)*

GEOFFREY. *(looking into cot)* You'll never know what I've been through will you, little man? *(BABY chuckles happily.)* One day maybe you'll be an M.P. like Daddy. And if you are, let's hope you can catch the Speaker's eye. *(A rattle shoots out of the carry cot, hitting GEOFFREY.)* That's a good one. I'll remember that!! *(He hurries upstairs.)*

(PATEL & MRS. WAYNEFLETE enter.)

PATEL. I'm glad you found the book. I shall greatly miss those readings of yours.

MRS. W. So shall I. I was very happy here with my books and those lovely old films. And with your splendid company it all seemed so civilized.

PATEL. I too am feeling the same.

MRS. W. I suppose we couldn't continue the cruise?

PATEL. A ship like this would cost a lot to run.

MRS. W. I have quite a bit of money put aside in the Building Society, and I shall charter it.

PATEL. What -- all of it?

MRS. W. We shall stay on, you as the Captain and I as your passenger.

PATEL. Oh, I would love that, but is it possible?

MRS. W. Anything is possible, if you see life as I do.

PATEL. You will read to me every night and we will play cards.

MRS. W. And you will continue to appraise me of the weather and our various ports of call.

PATEL. Frequently, frequently. And you will dress like this for dinner every night.

MRS. W. As long as I'm at your table.

PATEL. You are always at the top of my list. *(Starts to go.)*

MRS. W. Where are you going?

PATEL. To cancel my milk.

MRS. W. Not now. Sit down and join me in a game of cards.

PATEL. Thank you. *(He joins her.)*

MRS. W. It's such a relief now that the storm is over.

PATEL. Yes indeed. We have a saying in our country, "wonderful boating weather" — we even have a song about it. *(Starts to sing the Eton Boating Song.)*
PULL, PULL TOGETHER...
MRS. W. *(Sings.)*
FEATHERS ON THE BLADE.
PATEL. *(joyously)* Oh, you know it.
MRS. W. Yes. *(Continues.)*
WONDERFUL BOATING WEATHER...
BOTH.
SHANDY AND LEMONADE.

CURTAIN FALLS

FURNITURE LIST

Armchair
Wall seat/table
Wooden stool
Metal table
Perspex top
Long green cushion
Small green cushion
3 blue cushions
2 boxes glued together
Tea chest
Fridge freezer
Cooker
Cooker top
Sink unit
Bowl
Tap
Water pump (own box)
Barstool
4 kitchen stools
Kitchen table
False table top
Kitchen chair & cushion
Tin bath of peat
Tea chest of rocks

ACT I PRESET

KITCHEN

Deep Freeze:
in it: packets of food (leave room for bread)
on it: washing up bowl, in it: tea towel, rubber gloves, Fairy liquid

Fridge:
in it: 2 empty ice trays, bottle of milk, dressing
above it: hook for letters
on it: cushion with velcro strip US

Table:
on it: Times, magazine SR end, fruit bowl
under it: stools

Bar flap down:
OP shelf from DS:
Bottom shelf: bottle opener, whiskey, Bristol milk, soda syphon, Bristol dry, spirit bottle, dressing
2nd shelf: 6 champagne glasses, Remy Martin, Moet, Tio Pepe, martini, gin, soft drink dressing, spirit bottle dressing
3rd shelf: soft drink & spirit dressing

PS shelf from DS:
Bottom shelf: 2 champagne & sherry glasses, stoppered bottles, 2 racks Moet & Chandon
2nd shelf: 2 cans beer, whisky tumblers, brandy glasses 1 full wine rack

3rd shelf: Paris goblets, beer glasses, Wellington 8 oz
Centre shelf from PS to OP:
Bottom shelf: tonic water, bitter lemon, ginger ale (3
    deep — 2 layers)
2nd shelf: 6 Romanoff, 6 Grouse, 6 Gordon's (all 2X3
    deep) 1 full wine rack
3rd shelf: 1 full wine rack, wine bottle, full rack
4th shelf: tins of beers: 2 lager, 3 light ale, 3 lager, 4
    shandy, 1 lager, 1 light ale
on floor: empty & full crates under shelves
CHECK: bar door down
Work top/sink/cooker:
electric kettle (full) & lead (out), bovril, coffee, 3 tea tins,
    powdered milk, tin foil, sink tidy & brush, 4 mugs on
    mug tree
above it: kitchen towel on holder (facing out)
Drawers:
top drawer: cutlery, soil cloth
2nd drawer: green tablecloth
Cupboard:
waste bucket — empty
CHECK: cupboards shut
S/R Shelves (DS to US):
section 1:
3 patterned cannisters, blue kitchen utensil holder &
    utensils
section 2:
bottom shelf: pile of 6 dinner plates, 7 side plates & 1 tea
    knife, pile of 8 saucers
2nd shelf: blue casserole dish, blue salad shaker
3rd shelf: 3 striped jars, 1 larger striped jar

section 3:

on shelf: clear plastic jug behind 2 matching tumblers, butter dish behind sugar bowl, 8 cups — piled 2 high — behind 2 piles of 2 cups & saucers & teaspoons, 2 extra teaspoons

above shelf: 2 blue wire racks with 1 basket each

1st rack: fork with wooden handle, fish slice with wooden handle, ladel with wooden handle, strainer with wooden handle

in basket: steel tongs

2nd rack: wire whisk, wire slicer, in basket: grater

hanging under basket: red plastic jug, red plastic tongs

hanging at side: oven gloves

section 4:

2 red mats on them: blue biscuit tin, vase (empty)

CHECK:

> *earth in wall*
> *pin in door*
> *SR shelves in*
> *water works — pump water up*
> *waste disposal unit closed*
> *drawers shut*
> *hatch catch*

HALLWAY

S/R WALL (US to DS):

on DS doorpost: oxygen gauge, above it: pad with list & pen

tea chest, in it: 1 saucepan, 1 ashtray, wrapped in newspaper

US of it: 1 deep freeze cushion

on it: 1 deep freeze
1 cardboard box, in it: glass water jug (wrapped in paper), 2 figurines (wrapped in paper), ice bucket, lid
1 cardboard box, closed
CHECK fridge & freezer open, hook
S/L WALL (US to DS):
CHECK lever — Pin In!
1 box of video films inc. "Mrs. Minniver"
1 cardboard box, closed
2 solid boxes on top of each other, glued together
1 cardboard box, closed

LIVING ROOM

S/L Shelves (US to DS):
in recess: crocodile clip
in cupboard: travelling rug
bottom shelf: amplifier, on it: headphones & paperbacks US
2nd shelf: Hi-fi, video
3rd shelf: record & sleeve, TV
top shelf: paperbacks, speaker
D/S Wall:
radio & microphone
stool (DSL corner)
US/L Table:
pen holder & pens
table lamp
photo of baby
U/S Wall
map — check fixing nails

cushion — on wall seat
cushion — middle of wall seat
CHECK fail safe hatch closed
Coffee table

D.S.P.S. PROPS TABLE:
orange box containing: torch, white water bottle, grey
    bottle, water bottle, orange survival bag
hurricane lamp
3 clean dessert spoons
1 dirty dessert spoon (custard)
campbed & bedding with: "Jane Eyre" — open face up
    playing cards
Deirdre's handbag

U.S.P.S. PROPS TABLE:
telephone engineer's bag with: tools in leather wallet
    (wire cutters), white phone, black phone, broken coin-
    box, docket & pen on board, 6 ft. white cable
    (coiled)
spare docket & pen
5-6 magazines
2 hardbacked books
wall calendar & pen
pannier containing: nappy box, 2 boxes for baby
    bottles
pile of records
4 loaves of bread in carrier bag
green phone with cable
½ full feeding bottle
empty feeding bottle

log book & pen

TOP LEVEL PROPS TABLE:
golf clubs, golf cap in front pocket
   6 iron centre — diamond cap
   8 iron left — "2" cap
carrycot containing full feeding bottle
reel of cable *(CHECK it has been rejoined)* fixed to flat
daffodils
letters (4) & gas bill

O.P. PROPS TABLE:
Krug bottle (filled)
Champagne glass
2 bent spoons
⅓ pt. milk
fuller's earth
2 fancy plastic glasses
bottle of green drink
electric fan
box of dust & container
plate & fork
cling film
false table top; on it:
   cloth & 4 bowls of sponge pudding, 4 dessert spoons, 4
   mugs with dregs

DSR:
tin bath & box for earth

PERSONAL PROPS

GEOFFREY — pen, spectacles, wristwatch

MRS. W. — spectacles, handkerchief, red bag (in it: 2 £5 notes, mirror), evening bag (in it: coins), holdall, parasol, Forsyte Saga

JOE — wristwatch, 4 playing cards (3 clubs, 9 diamonds, queen hearts, & ace)

PATEL — wristwatch, Munta beads, Krishna picture, money bag, milkman's book, pencil, note to milkman, notes & coins

RAYMOND — key & chain, wallet

POLICEMAN — pad & pen, pad of parking tickets

SONIA — handbag, compact & lipstick

INTERVAL CHANGE

KITCHEN:
strike:

> flowers from vase
> carrier bag
> money
> ice bucket
> glass jug
> dirty cups, glasses and spoons

set:

> cutlery under bowl in sink
> 2 spoons (1 custardy) — in bowl
> 2 spoons — S/L of sink
> 6 champagne glasses — S/L of sink
> Remy Martin — U/S of champagne glasses
> log book — S/R end of table

reset:

> sugar bowl — to S/R shelves
> magazine & newspaper — into box in hall (DS/R)
> bar stool — to DS/R of bar flap

HALL:
strike:

> box DS/L

set:

> 3 trays tinned food — DS/R
> 2 bowls pudding & spoons — in tea chest

survival box, survival bag
torch, hurricane lamp, 2 bottles — DS/L
golf cap — sticking out of front pocket of golf bag

reset:
lever — DS of golf bag

LIVING ROOM:
strike:
ashtray
mug
rug
umbrella
telephone cable
magazines

set:
"Ideal Home" mag — US/L table
carrycot — US seat (head S/L)

ASM PROPS — ACTION LIST

Pre-show:
collect ice & set on stage
fill kettle with boiling water

ACT I:
clear pannier from DS/L
boil kettle for interval

Interval Change:

ACT II:
      wash up before spoons cue
      spoons cue
      glass of Krug champagne & bottle
      collect 2 glasses
      hand 2 plastic glasses
      assist costume change — powder
      hand milk bottle
      refill champagne bottle
      handbag into carrycot

Scene Change:

End of show:
      2 tablecloths & earth cloth — to laundry
      audio visual equipment to secure place
      holdall to dressing room

SCENE CHANGE LIST

A.S.M.
set:
      tray — on bar stool
      2 brandy glasses — DS/L of sink
      chair — S/R of table

strike:
      dirty glasses

Krug bottle
baby bottle
spoons (onto tray)
tablecloth
log book

reset:
Tio Pepe — in bar

PROP MAN 1:
move furniture in kitchen to ACT I marks
strike: tray of glasses — from bar stool

PROP MAN 2:
clear earth & rocks
set: false table top

PROP MAN 3:
clear earth & rocks
set: false table top, carrycot on freezer (head D/S)
strike: tin bath, soil cloth

PROP MAN 4:
bring on tin bath
sweep up
set: DS/R stool is DS/R recess
lock S/L door
exit S/L & give clearance

PROP MAN 5:
set:

campbed — DS/C of hall
pillow — S/L end of bed
book — on pillow
handbag on freezer

reset:

coffee table to S/L of armchair
stool to S/L of table
cards on table

strike:

sherry glass
"Forsyte" book

PROPS MAN ACTION LIST

ACT I
USR Q1 — bar door out

INTERVAL

USR Q1 — kitchen shelves off
USR Q3 — earth truck off
DSR Q2 — push hatch door open (with maroon), blow
dust through hatch

SCENE CHANGE

DSR Q3 — pin out of hatch catch

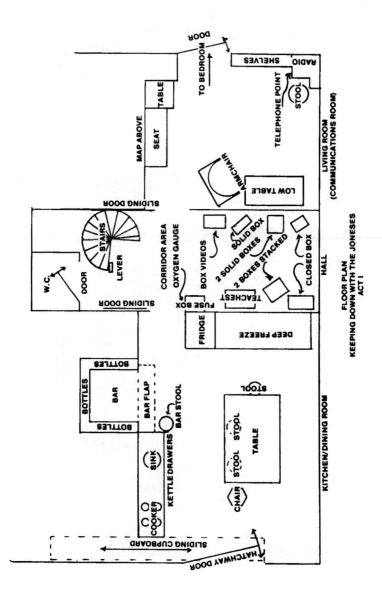

FLOOR PLAN
KEEPING DOWN WITH THE JONESES
ACT I

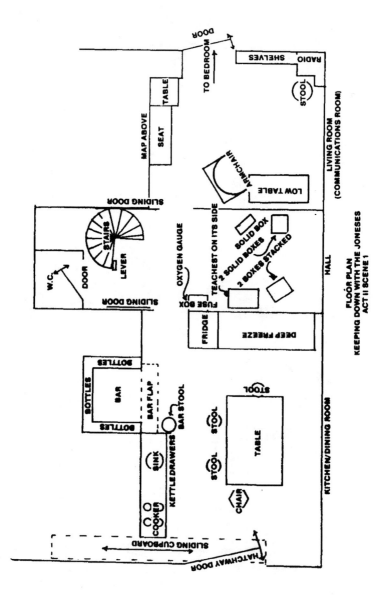

FLOOR PLAN
KEEPING DOWN WITH THE JONESES
ACT II SCENE 1

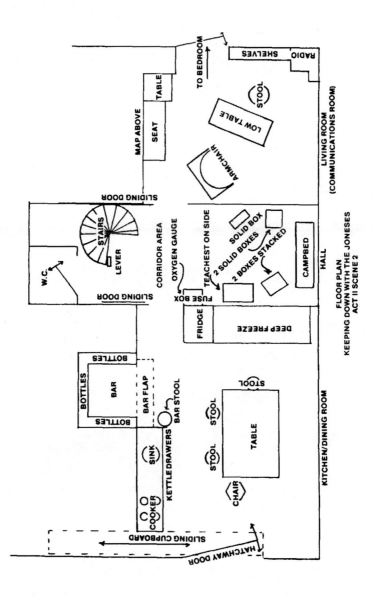

FLOOR PLAN
KEEPING DOWN WITH THE JONESES
ACT II SCENE 2